FIGHTING FOR THEIR COUNTRY: MINORITIES AT WAR

Minority Soldiers Fighting in the Korean War

DEREK MILLER

Cavendish Square
New York

Published in 2018 by Cavendish Square Publishing, LLC
243 5th Avenue, Suite 136, New York, NY 10016

Copyright © 2018 by Cavendish Square Publishing, LLC

First Edition

No part of this publication may be reproduced, stored in a retrieval system, or transmitted in any form or by any means—electronic, mechanical, photocopying, recording, or otherwise—without the prior permission of the copyright owner. Request for permission should be addressed to Permissions, Cavendish Square Publishing, 243 5th Avenue, Suite 136, New York, NY 10016. Tel (877) 980-4450; fax (877) 980-4454.

Website: cavendishsq.com

This publication represents the opinions and views of the author based on his or her personal experience, knowledge, and research. The information in this book serves as a general guide only. The author and publisher have used their best efforts in preparing this book and disclaim liability rising directly or indirectly from the use and application of this book.

CPSIA Compliance Information: Batch #CS17CSQ

All websites were available and accurate when this book was sent to press.

Library of Congress Cataloging-in-Publication Data

Names: Miller, Derek.
Title: Minority soldiers fighting in the Korean War / Derek Miller.
Description: New York : Cavendish Square, 2018. | Series: Fighting for their country: minorities at war | Includes index.
Identifiers: ISBN 9781502626653 (library bound) | ISBN 9781502626592 (ebook)
Subjects: LCSH: Korean War, 1950-1953--Juvenile literature. | African American soldiers--Juvenile literature. | African American soldiers--History--20th century--Juvenile literature.
Classification: LCC DS918.M52 2018 | DDC 951.904'2--dc23

Editorial Director: David McNamara
Editor: Caitlyn Miller
Copy Editor: Alex Tessman
Associate Art Director: Amy Greenan
Designer: Stephanie Flecha
Production Coordinator: Karol Szymczuk
Photo Research: J8 Media

The photographs in this book are used by permission and through the courtesy of: Cover Carl Mydans/The LIFE Picture Collection/Getty Images; p. 4 Corporal Peter McDonald, USMC/Wikimedia Commons/File:Chosin.jpg/CCO; p. 8 U.S. National Archives and Records Administration/Wikimedia Commons/File:Warkorea American Soldiers.jpg/CCO; pp. 10, 14, 17, 29, 31 Bettmann/Getty Images; p. 12 US Census Bureau/Wikimedia Commons/File:GreatMigration1910to1970-UrbanPopulation.png/CCO; p. 22 Afro Newspaper/Gado/Archive Photos/Getty Images; p. 26 Cameron Davidson/Corbis Documentary/Getty Images; p. 36 The U.S. Army Center of Military History/Wikimedia Commons/File:Race to Yalu Map.gif/CCO; p. 39 Sovfoto/Universal Images Group/Getty Images; p. 42 Universal Images Group/Getty Images; p. 44 Alfred Eisenstaedt/The LIFE Picture Collection/Getty Images; p. 48 Wikimedia Commons/File:Douglas MacArthur inspecting 24th infantry at Kimpo HD-SN-99-03034.JPEG/CCO; p. 52 US Army/Wikimedia Commons/File:24th Inf Howitzer.jpg/CCO; p. 56 United States Army/Wikimedia Commons/File:William H. Thompson (MOH).jpg/CCO; p. 58 U.S. military/Wikimedia Commons/File:Cornelius Charlton.jpg/CCO; p. 60 U.S. Navy/Wikimedia Commons/File:Jesse L Brown USN.jpg/CCO; p. 65 Dominic D'Andrea, commissioned by the National Guard Heritage Foundation/Wikimedia Commons/File:US 65th Infantry Regiment.Painting.Korean War.Bayonet charge against Chinese division.jpg/CCO; p. 67 United States Army/Wikimedia Commons/File:Juan-negron-united-states-army-medal-of-honor.jpg/CCO; p. 71 Wikimedia Commons/File:Capt. Manuel J. Fernandez Jr. of the 34th Fighter Intercepter Wing.jpg/CCO; p. 72 Unknown Marine/Wikimedia Commons/File:Lopez scaling seawall.jpg/CCO; p. 76 Corbis Historical/Getty Images; p. 81 ©AP Images; p. 85 Saul Loeb/AFP/Getty Images; p. 88 Stock Montage/Archive Photos/Getty Images; p. 91 Howard Sochurek/The LIFE Picture Collection/Getty Images; p. 92 Robert W. Kelley/The LIFE Picture Collection/Getty Images; p. 94 Anthony Barboza/Archive Photos/Getty Images.

Printed in the United States of America

CONTENTS

INTRODUCTION:
The Cold War Warms Up............**5**

1. Life at Home......................**11**
2. The War—Tragedies and Triumphs.....**27**
3. The 24th Infantry Regiment..........**49**
4. Hispanic Soldiers and
   Stories of Heroism................**65**
5. Changing Times **81**

Glossary.........................**98**
Bibliography **102**
Further Information...............**105**
Index **108**
About the Author **112**

INTRODUCTION

The Cold War Warms Up

On June 25, 1950, the Korean People's Army (**KPA**) of North Korea invaded South Korea without warning. The US-backed Republic of Korea (ROK) Army was no match for the well-prepared and well-armed KPA. The South Koreans were quickly pushed down the Korean peninsula and the South Korean capital of **Seoul** fell within three days. It looked like the war would be over shortly, but US President Harry S. Truman decided to intervene in the conflict. The American armed forces quickly made their way to Korea and managed to stop the onslaught of communist forces just before the South Koreans were driven into the sea. Defeat had narrowly been prevented in the opening months of the war, but there would still be much fighting to come.

Over the next three years, fighting would ravage almost the entire peninsula as the two opposing armies struggled to defeat one another. **UN** forces would push the KPA almost to

Opposite: US Marines prepare to engage Chinese forces in the frozen landscape of North Korea.

the Chinese border at the northern end of the peninsula before China intervened and once again drove them back. Seoul would fall yet again, but it was liberated a second time. Eventually, peace was agreed upon with virtually the same border as at the beginning of the war. Despite the deaths of some five million people in the fighting, the peninsula remained divided along the same line.

While neither side achieved their objective of uniting the Korean peninsula, the war had lasting consequences. The vibrant, democratic nation of South Korea that exists today is a direct result of the actions of many soldiers from around the globe who fought to stop the spread of communism. Soldiers from the United States, Canada, Australia—and South Korea itself—fought bravely so that future generations could live outside of the totalitarian state that still controls North Korea today.

The Korean War is sometimes called the Forgotten War. The larger conflict of World War II that preceded it by just a few years is given much more attention in history classes around the world. In the United States, the Vietnam War that followed the Korean War left a more lasting impression on popular consciousness. But the Korean War was an important conflict in the history of the twentieth century. It was the first time that the United States decided to commit American soldiers to stop the spread of communism around the world. It was a decision that would later set a precedent for the Vietnam War and make it clear to the world that the United States would not stand idly by while communism and totalitarianism spread around the globe.

However, the story of the Korean War is a somewhat difficult one for many reasons. In the early days of the war, the US Army was nearly defeated. For reasons we will soon see, the American troops were poorly equipped and trained when they first arrived in Korea. This led to a series of stinging defeats. While white units were soon forgiven, African American units and individuals were scapegoated. The 24th Infantry Regiment—composed of black soldiers—was disbanded as a result of their performance under fire, despite the fact that many white units behaved similarly and were not disbanded. In the racially charged atmosphere of that time, the failure of African American units was blamed on their race. Alternatively, the failure of white units was blamed on the real reasons, such as inadequate training, leadership, and equipment.

It was only recently in 1996—more than forty years after the war ended—that the United States Army released a report vindicating the 24th Infantry Regiment. It placed the blame for the poor performance of the 24th squarely on the shoulders of the army command rather than the black soldiers who served their country bravely. It concluded that not only did the 24th have to contend with inadequate training, leadership, and equipment, it also faced racial prejudice within the army that led to a breakdown of trust between the soldiers and their superior officers. This had negative consequences on the battlefield, despite many acts of individual bravery and valor by African American soldiers.

Spurred by the dissolution of the 24th, the US Army fully integrated for the first time in its history during the Korean War. Whites, African Americans, Hispanics, Native Americans, and other minorities fought shoulder to shoulder in defense

Minority soldiers who fought in integrated units returned home to a segregated country.

of freedom and democracy. However, equality was still out of reach for many Americans at home during the Korean War. Segregation was still the law of the land in the United States, and minorities were treated as second-class citizens. Movie theaters, water fountains, and even hospitals were segregated according to race. While these facilities were supposed to be of equal quality, that was almost never the case. Minorities were forced to use substandard facilities across the United States—particularly in the South—due to the color of their skin.

We will examine the actions and legacy of the 24th Infantry Regiment as well as minority soldiers in other units. A number of minority soldiers were awarded the Medal of Honor and other decorations for their heroic actions during the Korean War. Even though their war may be called the Forgotten War in the United States, their bravery and courage are a credit to their country. The people of South Korea have never forgotten their sacrifice that made the free and democratic nation of South Korea possible.

Life at Home

American society in the 1940s and 1950s was rampant with racial inequality, discrimination, segregation, and sometimes racial violence. Minorities often found themselves besieged by hostile neighbors, state governments, and the federal government. The promise of the Declaration of Independence—that "all men are created equal"—was still just a dream.

JIM CROW

African Americans were subject to unequal treatment across the United States and especially in the South. **Jim Crow laws** that legislated racial segregation were common in Southern states. Blacks were forbidden from using the same facilities as whites. They were forced to attend separate schools, which were underfunded and derelict. They were also often not afforded

Opposite: Segregated facilities, like this one in Florida, were typical in the years before the Korean War.

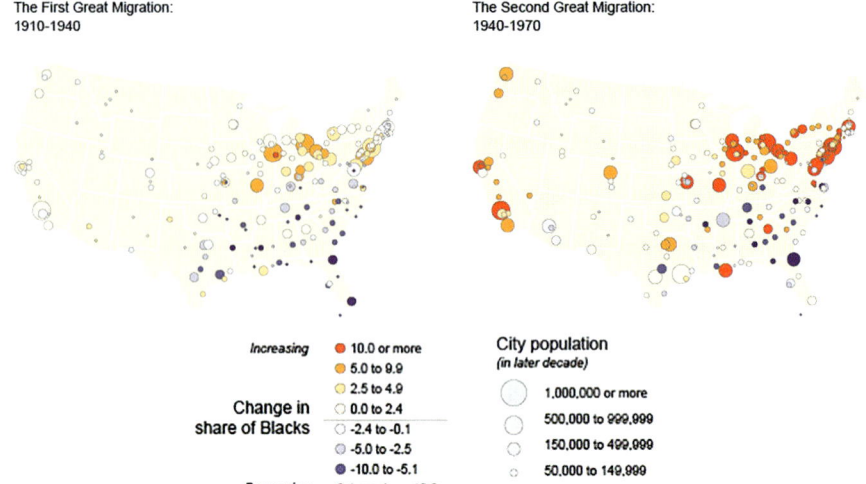

During the Great Migration, African Americans left the South for cities in the North and West in huge numbers.

the protection of the law and were unjustly imprisoned and convicted of crimes due to the color of their skin.

Jim Crows laws were also responsible for the **disenfranchisement** of many African Americans in the South. The Fifteenth Amendment guaranteed African Americans the right to vote and was passed in 1870. However, many Southern states had found ways to undermine the amendment. Measures such as poll taxes and literacy tests were passed by state legislatures. These unfairly targeted African Americans, who were generally less wealthy and less educated due to the racial discrimination and segregation of the times. Often the laws were specially crafted to guarantee that poor, illiterate white Southerners could still vote. As a result, state governments and Congressional representatives from the South were almost entirely white, despite the large percentage of African Americans in the region.

Historically, Jim Crow laws were often supported by racial violence and terror. For many years, violent white supremacist groups such as the Ku Klux Klan terrorized African American communities in the South. Lynchings and mob violence ensured that African Americans could not protest for equal rights. This caused a large migration of African Americans out of the rural South to cities in the West (notably in California) and the North, such as Chicago, New York, and Detroit. This demographic shift, known as the **Great Migration**, took place over six decades between 1910 and 1970.

However, by the 1950s, racial violence had decreased significantly in the United States. According to statistics kept by the Tuskegee Institute, 1952 saw no lynchings in the United States. This was the first year with no lynchings since the Tuskegee Institute began keeping track in 1882. For comparison, in 1933 an estimated twenty-four African Americans were lynched. They died at the hands of white mobs for suspected crimes or simply not showing whites the respect they thought they were due.

Emmett Till

Even though the number of lynchings had fallen to record lows in the early 1950s, savage acts of racial violence still took place. One of the most famous victims was fourteen-year-old Emmett Till. Born in Chicago, Till left his home in the North one summer to visit his extended family in Alabama. His mother told him before he left on his trip that things were different in the South. She told him that he should get down on his knees and beg forgiveness of a white person if they asked. But her advice could not save Emmett Till from the injustices of the

Emmett Till's murder shocked the country.

South. He was kidnapped, tortured, and murdered in Alabama for allegedly whistling at a white woman in a store.

The lynching of Emmett Till would be famous around the country and helped to inspire future civil rights leaders. His mother insisted on an open casket funeral so that people could see what had been done to her son. Photographs of his body were published in magazines and newspapers. African Americans around the country called for justice. These calls would galvanize a generation of activists. Yet though the two men who killed Emmett Till were put on trial, the all-white jury found them not guilty after just an hour of deliberation. The two men later confessed to the killing. However, they were never punished for the crime.

UNEQUAL TREATMENT UNDER THE LAW

Even though lynchings had declined by the 1950s, African Americans were often discriminated against. In many cases, it was the criminal justice system that treated them unfairly, going so far as to unjustly kill them. The overbearing criminal justice system was part of the institutional restriction of the civil rights and human rights of African Americans at the time. African Americans faced far harsher sentences for crimes than their white counterparts. The law was also twisted to harass and silence African Americans who protested the injustices of the era.

One of the most outrageous injustices of the 1950s was the case of Jeremiah Reeves, an African American man from Alabama. Reeves was just sixteen years old when he was arrested for allegedly raping a white woman. Despite little evidence and the likelihood that any romance was consensual, Reeves was quickly convicted by an all-white jury and sentenced to death. The US Supreme Court overturned the conviction because the jury had not been informed that Reeves's confession had been obtained under duress: interrogators had taken him to the state death chamber to threaten him during questioning. Nevertheless, the second all-white jury convicted Reeve just the same, even after hearing the circumstances of his confession.

Despite the actions of civil rights leaders who worked on his behalf, Jeremiah Reeves was executed on March 28, 1958. It was clear that even in 1950s, justice could not be counted on for African Americans in the South. Days after the execution, Martin Luther King Jr. denounced the event in a speech at the state capitol of Alabama:

> *A young man, Jeremiah Reeves, who was little more than a child when he was first arrested, died in the electric chair for the charge of rape. Whether or not he was guilty*

of this crime is a question that none of us can answer. But the issue before us now is not the innocence or guilt of Jeremiah Reeves. Even if he were guilty, it is the severity and inequality of the penalty that constitutes the injustice. Full grown white men committing comparable crimes against Negro girls are rarely ever punished, and are never given the death penalty or even a life sentence. It was the severity of Jeremiah Reeves penalty that aroused the Negro community, not the question of his guilt or innocence.

Race Riots

In addition to miscarriages of justice, so-called race riots were also a venue for violence against African Americans in this period. Many race riots began when whites victimized an African American and ended with white police officers using excessive force against black crowds.

In the Colombia Race Riot of 1946, a fight between a black veteran and a white veteran led to rumors of a lynch mob and the wounding of white police officers. A large contingent of police officers went into the African American neighborhood and arrested more than a hundred men. In police custody, two of the men were shot—the only two deaths of the "race riot." The police claim that the men had seized weapons in custody was viewed with skepticism.

JACKIE ROBINSON

Until 1947, professional sports in the United States were segregated. African Americans and whites were not allowed to play against one another. That all changed on April 15, 1947, when Jackie Robinson played his first game for the Brooklyn Dodgers. His debut marked the end of the unofficial policy of racial segregation in Major League Baseball. Although he would suffer years of abuse from fans, rival teams, and even

Jackie Robinson in 1953—one of the five years he played in the MLB All-Star Game

some of his own teammates, Jackie Robinson persevered and continued playing for the Dodgers for nine years.

Throughout his career, Robinson earned a number of distinctions. He was named the MLB Rookie of the Year in 1947. He also helped the Dodgers win the World Series in 1955. In addition to his successful career in baseball, Robinson was also a prominent advocate for civil rights for African Americans. He served on the board of the National Association for the Advancement of Colored People (**NAACP**) and spoke out publicly for greater integration in sports. Jackie Robinson's breaking of the color line in baseball inspired African Americans across the United States. It challenged the status quo of racial segregation. Robinson used his fame as a force for change.

NATIVE AMERICAN "TERMINATION POLICY"

Yet African Americans were not the only group to face inequality and injustice. Native Americans have suffered a great deal throughout the history of the United States. This is true of the time period before and during the Korean War as well. After forcing Native Americans from their ancestral lands and onto small reservations for much of American history, the United States government began to take away even these reservations during the 1940s. This was part of an attempt to force Native Americans to assimilate to mainstream society at the cost of their cultural identity.

The US government of the time labelled this policy the "Termination Policy." Tribes that had existed for centuries were terminated with a stroke of the pen. Their rights and lands were taken away and the legal basis of their tribal identity destroyed. Between the years of 1953 and 1964, 109 different

Native American tribes were terminated by the government—a devastating blow to their cultural identity and history as well as their land rights.

This was not the only injustice that Native Americans suffered in the twentieth century. From the late nineteenth century until 1929, many Native American children were forced to attend boarding schools. At these schools, they were often physically abused and forced to renounce their culture—students caught using their tribal languages were punished harshly. Although efforts were made to change these inhumane practices beginning in 1929, they were not always successful. Native American culture was taught briefly in the schools, but by 1945, conservatives had largely undermined this effort in favor of increased "assimilation."

One of the main reasons for the termination policy and efforts at assimilation during the 1940s and 1950s was the terrible conditions found on many reservations. Decades of mismanagement by the Bureau of Indian Affairs had left Native Americans impoverished and neglected with no opportunities to improve their lives. The government did not provide more resources to right this injustice. Instead, government officials tried to force Native Americans off their reservations to join mainstream American society.

DISCRIMINATION AGAINST HISPANIC AMERICANS

Hispanic Americans would also face intense racial discrimination during the time of the Korean War and the years preceding it. For Hispanics, schools and other public facilities were segregated in some parts of the country just as they were for African Americans. This only began to change in 1947 with the important court case of **Mendez v. Westminster**. For the first time in US history, a judge ruled that segregation was unconstitutional. Orange County in California was ordered to stop sending Mexican and white children to different schools based on the color of their skin. It took seven years before the Supreme Court ruled the same way regarding African American children being segregated in schools.

But segregation was not the only hardship that Hispanics faced in the first half of the twentieth century. Like African Americans, they also had to contend with racial violence. One famous outbreak of violence against Mexican Americans was the Zoot Suit Riots of 1943 that took place in Los Angeles, California. White soldiers stationed in L.A. during World War II clashed with Mexican American youths in zoot suits—a kind of oversized suit that was popular at the time. Sparked by a late-night fight between a group of soldiers and youths, the violence dragged on for days. Mexican American youths as young as twelve were stripped and beaten in the streets of the city. The police often declined to intervene in the violence that was instigated by white soldiers. Finally, servicemen were banned from entering L.A. Zoot suits were banned in the city to stop the violence.

In addition to segregation and racial violence, Mexican Americans also faced the prospect of deportation in the 1930s and 1940s. The fact that many were US citizens and born within the United States did not prevent them from being forced from the country. As many as two million people were deported in this twenty-year period. The majority of the deported were American citizens. Many families were broken apart. Children were separated from their parents and parents from their children. Sometimes, they would never be able to find one another again.

RACE AND THE COLD WAR

The harsh treatment of minorities within the United States became an international issue during the Cold War. The Soviet Union and United States were locked in a conflict for influence around the world. They both tried to promote their competing ideologies of communism and democracy to nations around the globe—especially in Africa, Asia, and South America. The Soviet Union utilized the treatment of African Americans as a source of propaganda. Repeated civil rights violations in the United States against people of color hurt the image of the United States abroad. They also sowed mistrust between foreign leaders and the leaders in Washington. One of the most famous cases that gained international notoriety was that of Jimmy Wilson.

In 1958, Jimmy Wilson, an African American man, was put on trial for stealing $1.95 from a white woman. An all-white jury convicted him and sentenced him to death. While robbery was a capital crime then, no white man had ever been sentenced to death for it. Only four African American men had previously been executed for the crime. Furthermore, the amount of money stolen had never before been so small. Jimmy Wilson appealed his conviction to the Supreme Court of Alabama, which decided that there was no evidence of unfair treatment and upheld the death penalty. If mercy for Jimmy Wilson was to occur, it appeared it must come from

Minorities in World War II

The US Army that waged World War II was a segregated fighting force. African Americans were placed in all-black units with mostly white officers. They were also overwhelmingly placed into noncombat roles despite their desire to fight for their country. Most were relegated to important but thankless jobs in the army. These included supply and transportation roles. However, as the war dragged on, more and more African Americans found their way to the front lines to replace **casualties**. But even there they still served in segregated units

A group of Tuskegee Airmen in the United States before going to fight in Europe

and lived with discrimination. One of the most famous African American units of the war was the Tuskegee Airmen. These brave fighter plane pilots escorted American bombers over Europe during the war, engaging the feared German Luftwaffe in dogfights.

During the war, African American leaders at home started the Double V campaign. This movement called for two victories: the victory against fascism abroad and the victory against racism at home. While the United States prevailed against fascism overseas, the fight against racism would drag on for many decades. At the end of the war, the American armed forces were still segregated. At home, segregation also existed. It would be nine long years between the end of World War II and the Supreme Court decision *Brown v. Board of Education*. The case began the unravelling of segregation in the United States.

the governor of Alabama, James Folsom, who could commute the sentence to life imprisonment.

Communist newspapers around the world covered the case—pointing to the unfairness of the American system. At a time when the United States tried to portray itself abroad as a defender of human rights, the injustice of the sentence was a reminder of how far the country needed to come. As the Soviet Union and United States competed for influence in Africa and Asia, international incidents like Jimmy Wilson's conviction harmed the foreign policy of Washington, DC. As a result, the Secretary of State urged Governor Folsom to commute Wilson's sentence. He did so soon after the Supreme Court of Alabama rejected Wilson's appeal. People around the world rejoiced when they heard the governor listened and took the death penalty off the table. Yet many were shocked when they learned Wilson still faced a sentence of life imprisonment. Wilson would ultimately spend sixteen years incarcerated for his crime.

DESEGREGATION OF THE ARMED FORCES

It was in this context of the Cold War that President Harry S. Truman became a strong supporter of civil rights for African Americans. In 1946, he set up the President's Committee on Civil Rights to investigate what actions the government should take. The committee recommended that numerous actions be taken by the government to expand civil rights for minorities. As a result, President Truman tried to pass anti-lynching legislation to combat racial violence. However, Congress refused to pass the bill. The Democratic Party, which Truman himself belonged to, splintered due to his support of civil rights. Southern Democrats formed their own pro-segregation party and broke with the president.

With Congress blocking legislation to protect civil rights, Truman took what steps he could on his own. In 1948, Truman issued **Executive Order No. 9981**. This executive order desegregated the US military. There was significant resistance to the order from many military officers, and integration proved to be a slow process. When the Korean War began in 1950, there were still segregated units. However, by the end of the war in 1953, integration had been completed. For the first time in history, black and white Americans fought together as equals in all branches of the US military.

The successful integration of the armed forces would serve as an important precursor of integration throughout the United States. Integration of the military bolstered combat effectiveness and morale, rather than eroding them as some critics of integration believed would happen. This was a powerful testament to the advantages of integration over continued segregation. It also cemented President Truman's legacy as one of the most important presidents in the civil rights movement. In some ways, this seems unlikely. Truman had harbored racial prejudices in his early years. He was born in the South and his personal prejudices can be seen in his private letters from his youth. But his views changed later in life, especially after he witnessed the harsh treatment of African American veterans returning from World War II.

The War—Tragedies and Triumphs

It is impossible to understand the Korean War without examining the larger conflict it was part of—the Cold War. This struggle between the communist Soviet Union and democratic United States of America was a defining part of world history for forty-four years. From 1947 to 1991, countries and people around the world were dragged into the ideological struggle between the two superpowers. While it is called the Cold War because American and Soviet armies never met each other on the field of battle, many **proxy wars** were fought between the two countries. The Korean War and Vietnam War were the largest of these proxy wars. The Soviet Union did not deploy large numbers of troops in either war. The United States did.

Opposite: The Korean War Veterans Memorial in Washington, DC

Other conflicts took place around the globe in Africa, Asia, and Latin America. The Central Intelligence Agency (CIA) of the United States and their Soviet counterparts, the KGB, propped up regimes they deemed friendly and undermined regimes opposed to them.

In the end, the Soviet Union fell apart in 1991 due to a series of internal revolutions. The Cold War came to an end. Instead of two superpowers, only one remained: the United States. However, relics of the Cold War remain in the political structure of the world today. The North Atlantic Treaty Organization (NATO) was created to protect the free world from Soviet aggression. This organization still exists. NATO binds the US, Canada, and many European countries into an alliance obligated to help each other whenever a member state is attacked. The only time NATO has gone to war was the US-led war in Afghanistan. The war in Afghanistan began in 2001, some ten years after the end of the Cold War.

THE BEGINNING

The roots of the Cold War lie in the end of World War II. The United States and Soviet Union fought together against Nazi Germany and the Empire of Japan. In the peace that followed the war, the world was largely divided between the two victorious powers. Some countries were entirely within one power's **sphere of influence**. For instance, Japan was completely occupied by the United States. Alternatively, most of Eastern Europe, including Poland and Bulgaria, were puppet states of the Soviet Union. But other countries were split down the middle by the two powers. Germany and Korea were literally divided with pro-American and pro-Soviet regimes installed in their respective halves. This division of Korea would result in the Korean War: the first major conflict of the Cold War that American soldiers fought in.

Korea

The Korean Peninsula is a relatively small area of land in East Asia. It is about one and a half times the size of New York, although it is quite densely populated with more than triple New York's population. For much of history, Korea has been sandwiched between the much larger and more populous nations of Japan and China. These two powers have often tried to subjugate the smaller country of Korea. However, they rarely succeeded for long.

In 1910, Japan finally did manage to **annex** Korea. The Empire of Japan used Korea as a staging ground for its later invasions of China—a key theater of World War II. Japan would rule the Korean peninsula for thirty-five years, until it lost all of its mainland possessions with the conclusion of World War II. Though Japan was now unable to influence the future of the country, two new countries stepped into the power vacuum: the Soviet Union and United States. The conflict between the two

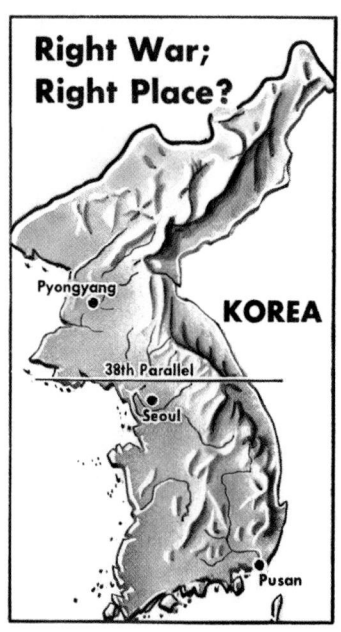

After World War II, Korea was divided along the 38th parallel.

The War—Tragedies and Triumphs 29

Park Chung Hee

In 1944, a Korean man by the name of Park Chung Hee graduated from a military academy in Manchuria—a region of northern China that was then under Japanese control. He was commissioned in the Manchurian army and served during the end of World War II with Chinese soldiers under Japanese command. He signed an oath of allegiance to the Japanese in his own blood to prove his loyalty. That oath was even published in a Japanese newspaper. At that time, Park Chung Hee was a minority soldier. Later in life he would change the course of his own country's history.

During the Korean War, he served in the South Korean army and rose through the ranks to become a brigadier general in 1953. After the war ended, he remained in the military. In 1961, he helped spearhead a coup that overthrew the democratic government of South Korea and gave power to the military. He soon seized power from the other planners of the coup and installed himself as president. He would remain in power for eighteen years until his assassination in 1979. Today, his legacy in South Korea is mixed. While the economy developed rapidly during his tenure, he mercilessly persecuted anyone who challenged his power. In 2013, his daughter Park Geun Hye was the first Korean woman to be inaugurated as president.

superpowers would drag Korea into the long and bloody war that would shape its history.

THE OUTBREAK OF HOSTILITIES

The North Korean invasion of South Korea in 1950 was an unprecedented escalation of Cold War tensions. The Cold War had only begun two years earlier. Until this point, the Cold War had simply consisted of both sides offering financial

Kim Il Sung ruled North Korea during the war. Today, his grandson Kim Jong Un is in control of the country.

support to sympathetic governments or rebels and the bloodless confrontation of the Berlin blockade. (The Soviet Union had blocked transportation into West Berlin which was under the control of the US and her allies. In response, the US airlifted supplies to the city for months before the blockade was lifted.) But with the invasion of South Korea, President Truman was confronted with a difficult choice. He had to either commit American soldiers to a distant war or watch from the sidelines as communism spread further across Asia by force.

In 1947, President Truman had laid forth his vision of American foreign policy during the Cold War. Now known as the **Truman Doctrine**, he advocated the United States work proactively to stop the spread of the Soviet Union by supporting countries under pressure from it. At the time, this largely consisted of sending financial aid to Greece and Turkey. But it was unclear if this strategy of **containment** would extend to sending American soldiers into Korea in 1950. President Truman decided in the early days of the war that it did. Therefore, he ordered American troops stationed in Japan to rush to the aid of South Korea.

The United Nations supported this action. It condemned the invasion of South Korea and passed a resolution calling for member states to aid the South Korean government. While the Soviet Union could have vetoed these actions by the UN, it was boycotting the UN at the time due to its refusal to recognize the communist government of China.

THE PUSAN PERIMETER

The first three months of the war were a disaster for South Korean and UN forces. The North Korean KPA was well equipped and ready for the war. They were outfitted with Soviet T–34 tanks and had prepared for the surprise attack that caught the South Koreans off guard. The KPA advanced quickly into South Korea. They took the capital of Seoul within a matter of days. South Korean forces were driven south across the Korea Peninsula in full retreat.

The war seemed lost until US troops began to arrive and reinforce the South Korean forces. The American troops—recently victorious in World War II—were expected to make short work of the KPA. But the US Army of 1950 was the not the army that had won World War II five years earlier. The number of American soldiers had shrunk from 12 million men to just 1.5 million in the past two years.

The American military was crippled by years of spending cuts. In the aftermath of World War II, the US government had focused on **nuclear deterrence** rather than maintaining a large, conventional fighting force. Policymakers believed that having an air force and nuclear bombs capable of destroying any other nation would prevent a ground war. The days of armies meeting on the field of battle was seen as a thing of the past. However, in a small proxy war, nuclear deterrence proved to be completely useless. The invasion of South Korea demanded the response of a conventional army. The undertrained and ill-equipped American soldiers in Japan were not prepared for the fight.

On July 5, 1950, American soldiers just south of Seoul made contact with the KPA for the first time. The engagement would come to be known as the Battle of Osan. The American troops found themselves facing a contingent of KPA supported by thirty-three T–34 tanks.

The bazookas of the American soldiers—meant to destroy or disable enemy tanks—bounced harmlessly off the sides of the T–34. Many of the American radios and machine guns were also not operational. The American soldiers were soon overrun. Enemy tanks pierced their line, and they were forced to retreat. The contingent of 540 American soldiers suffered more than 150 casualties and did little to delay the advancing KPA.

The Battle of Osan was typical of the early part of the Korean War. Unprepared American soldiers were thrown into combat against a numerically superior, battle-hardened enemy. The result was disastrous. Some three thousand Americans were killed, captured, or wounded in the first week of fighting in Korea. UN forces were unable to do more than slow down the advancing KPA. By August 4, 1950, just a month and a half after the start of the war, UN and South Korean forces were contained in a tiny pocket of land at the extreme southeast of the Korean Peninsula. They still held the important port city of **Pusan**, which was used to offload reinforcement and supplies to the surrounded army.

Over the next month and a half, the KPA attempted to breach the UN line. This line was known as the Pusan Perimeter, and the KPA wanted to cross it to drive the UN and South Korean forces into the sea. Meanwhile, the UN launched a number of counter-offensives to try to break out of their defensive positions. Their goal was to drive the KPA northward. In the end, the UN line held. The next chapter of the war would not be decided at the Pusan Perimeter, but two hundred miles to the north at the city of **Inchon**.

THE LANDING AT INCHON

UN forces were led by the American General Douglas MacArthur. MacArthur was famous for his leadership of a number of campaigns during World War II as well as his heading the American occupation of Japan after the war. A larger-than-life figure, MacArthur was extremely popular in the United States. However, conflicts with President Truman over the Korean War would later see him relieved of his command.

With UN and South Korean forces surrounded in the Pusan Perimeter, MacArthur planned a bold military maneuver to turn the tide of the war. Rather than try to break out of their position around Pusan, MacArthur decided to launch a surprise amphibious invasion behind enemy lines and retake Seoul. He convinced the other military leaders of the merits of his plan and set about preparing for the invasion. MacArthur decided that the landing should take place at Inchon, close to Seoul, despite the difficulties that the terrain presented there. The port was difficult to approach and had extreme tides, which made a landing difficult. Yet these conditions also increased the chance of a surprise attack, given the unlikelihood of a landing at that location.

On September 15, 1950, American troops landed at Inchon. Although resistance was fierce, the KPA were heavily outnumbered. In a matter of days, Inchon was captured and UN forces began advancing toward the capital of Seoul. During the Second Battle of Seoul, UN forces retook to city. The KPA was dangerously overextended. Their soldiers encircling the Pusan Perimeter were at risk of being cut off from North Korea and their already tenuous supply lines. A UN counter-attack at the Pusan Perimeter broke through the KPA line there and shattered the North Korean forces. Tens of thousands of KPA fighters were killed, captured, or deserted in their desperate retreat northward to avoid encirclement.

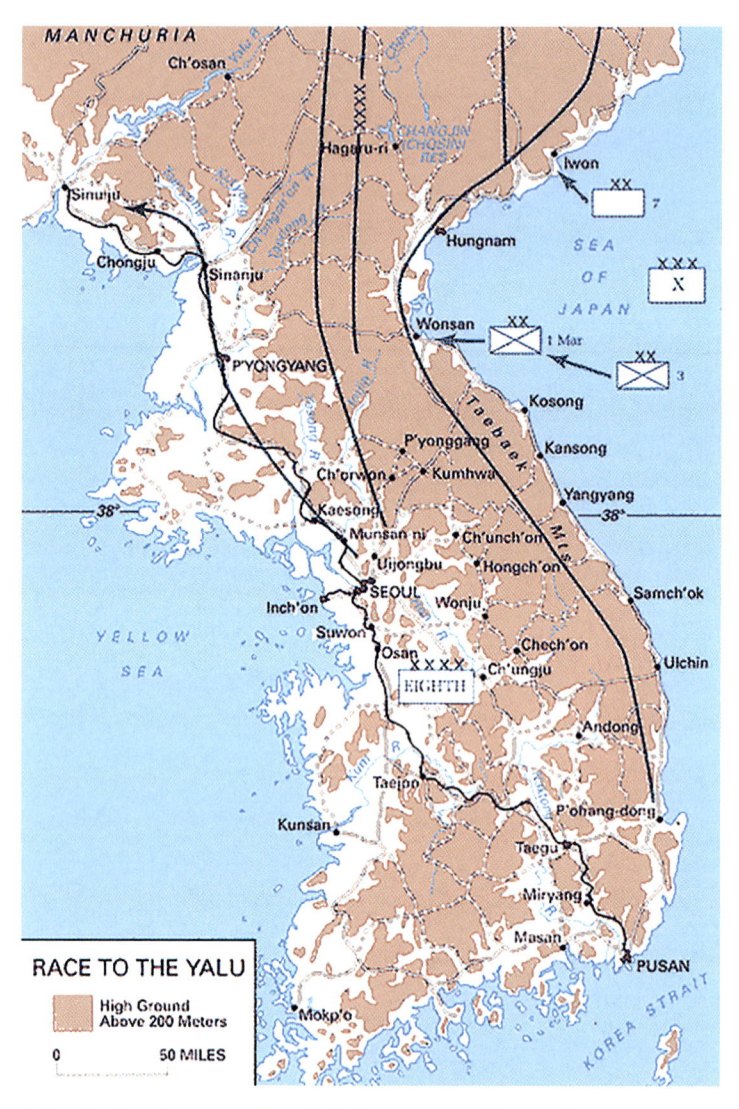

After the landing at Inchon, UN forces were able to advance all the way to the Yalu River—the border with China.

MacArthur's gamble had paid off. The landing at Inchon would be remembered as a stunning success in military history. It reversed the course of the war and delivered a much-needed victory to the UN forces. Morale soared to new heights as the soldiers who had been forced to retreat the entire war now pursued their enemies northward.

THE 38TH PARALLEL

By the end of September, 1950, South Korea was liberated. UN forces now faced an important choice in how to carry on with the war: should they cross over the **38th parallel** into North Korea or remain in South Korea? The US government believed that international law supported an invasion of North Korea because of the UN resolution that called for the defense of South Korea. However, there were still doubts as to whether crossing the 38th parallel was the wisest course of action. Until this point, both the Soviet Union and China had refrained from committing their own soldiers to battle. It remained to be seen if they would show the same restraint with an American army advancing toward their borders through North Korean territory.

MacArthur was a fierce advocate for a continued advance into North Korea all the way to the Yalu River—the border with China. He hoped to utterly destroy the **routed** KPA and unite the Korean Peninsula. In the end, President Truman and his administration agreed with MacArthur and gave him permission to pursue the KPA north of the 38th parallel. However, he was warned to stop his advance if it seemed like the Soviet Union or China was poised to enter the war.

UN forces swept into North Korea and drove the KPA northwards. **Pyongyang**, the capital of North Korea—soon fell to the advancing UN soldiers. It looked like the war was rapidly coming to a close and UN forces would be victorious. But on October 25, 1950, there was an ominous development. South Korean forces advancing in the northern reaches of North Korea reported that they had been ambushed by Chinese troops. Days later, American and Chinese soldiers clashed for the first time in battle.

The US government was unsure how to proceed given the Chinese intervention. European allies did not want war to expand with China or the Soviet Union because American forces were tied down in Korea. They feared the Soviet Union would be able to sweep across all of Europe if war broke out. On the other hand, General MacArthur argued that the UN should continue to advance all the way to the Yalu River. He said that anything less would make the United States appear weak. Other American policymakers wanted to stop the advance rather than risk antagonizing the Chinese. There were still doubts as to whether the Chinese intended to commit fully to the war or were simply trying to save face. These doubts were put to rest on November 25, 1950, when hundreds of thousands of Chinese soldiers launched a coordinated offensive against UN forces. Despite the early warnings that China was poised to enter the war, UN forces were caught off guard.

CHINA GOES TO WAR

A period of bitter fighting ensued between the exhausted UN forces and newly arrived Chinese soldiers. Conditions on the ground were extremely harsh in the mountainous terrain. Temperatures were often below 0 degrees Fahrenheit (-18 degrees Celsius). This led to many cases of frostbite and

Chinese soldiers cross the Yalu River into Korea on their way to fight UN forces.

difficulties maneuvering in deep snow and on icy roads. One of the most famous battle of the Korean War happened at this time: the **Battle of the Chosin Reservoir**.

Positioned around the frozen Chosin Reservoir in North Korea, fifteen thousand American soldiers—mostly US marines—were surrounded by advancing Chinese soldiers. Beset by overwhelming enemy forces and deadly cold, the surrounded marines fought for days to break out of the encirclement. Thousands of marines fought the enemy to withdraw along a narrow, icy road through the mountains. The 11-mile (17.7 kilometer) march lasted ninety-six hours and cost the lives of 1,100 marines. The battle would later come to be known as the "The Corp's Finest Hour." The survivors of the deadly fighting would be known as the Chosin Few.

US Army units involved in the battle also fought bravely but sustained a terrible number of casualties. Task Force Faith, a unit of 3,000 US Army soldiers, was reduced to just 385 men capable of fighting after the battle. The commander of the task force posthumously received the Medal of Honor for his actions during the battle. Many individual soldiers were awarded medals, too.

The legacy of the Chosin Reservoir is mixed. While it was one of the worst defeats in US military history, it could have been much worse. Through bravery and determination, thousands of US soldiers managed to fight their way out of encirclement and prevent themselves from being captured. This was lauded in the American press at the time. The failure of the Chinese to eliminate the fifteen thousand soldiers was a military disaster, despite their victory in the battle. Chinese forces also suffered many more casualties than UN forces, which hampered their continued advance in the coming months.

THE CHINESE ADVANCE

After the soldiers from the Chosin Reservoir were evacuated by the sea, the Chinese advance through North Korea continued. MacArthur did not have the necessary soldiers to stop the offensive. He warned that a complete withdrawal of UN forces from Korea might result if he were not reinforced with more men. While UN forces enjoyed complete control of the air and the ability to call in naval bombardments, the rough terrain of the Korean peninsula limited this advantage. Fighting was often in close quarters, and precise airstrikes were difficult in the rugged mountains. UN soldiers were weary from five months of fighting.

It was at this point that matters of international politics became front and center in the Korean War. General MacArthur believed that his ability to fight the war was being handicapped by the US government. Truman and his Cabinet refused to allow MacArthur to bomb Chinese bases in Manchuria—the Chinese region bordering North Korea. They worried that doing so would invite the Soviet Union to enter the conflict, sparking a world war. Western Europe was unprepared for a conventional war, and if the Soviet Union chose to it could easily seize all of Europe. This would be disastrous for the United States.

Even if the Soviet Union did not join the war, there were concerns that a long, drawn-out war with China would be a massive strategic error for the United States. While relatively inexpensive for China to send armies across their border with North Korea, the supplying of troops to distant South Korea was a huge expense for the United States. Communist China

Mao Zedong was the leader of China during the Korean War. His brutal reign is remembered for the deaths of tens of millions of Chinese civilians.

and the Soviet Union might take the opportunity to bleed the United States of its resources by dragging out a massive conventional war in Korea.

In the end, the Truman and his administration decided against any outright acts of aggression against China. Despite MacArthur's urgings, they would not allow him to destroy airfields in China or, as he wanted, bomb military factories and blockade the entire coast of China.

Chinese forces gradually pushed south, retaking Pyongyang and eventually taking Seoul on January 7, 1951. For the second time in the course of the war, the capital of South Korea fell to enemy forces. UN forces slowly retreated and plans were drawn up for a complete evacuation of the Korean Peninsula if it became necessary.

MacArthur's Dismissal

On April 11, 1951, General MacArthur was relieved of his command by President Truman. It proved to be one of the most controversial decisions of the war. Truman faced considerable criticism over it. MacArthur was a respected war hero and he enjoyed great popularity at home.

The reason for the dismissal was MacArthur's insistence that the Korean War be expanded to include mainland China as well. The disagreement between Truman and MacArthur about the scope of the war would have been acceptable behind closed doors. However, MacArthur was sometimes openly critical of the president's decisions. His statements to the press had bordered on criticism in the past. He also communicated with Republican Congressmen about how he thought the war should be fought—very differently from

General Douglas MacArthur in 1951—the year he was removed from command

how the president was doing it. In the end, Truman thought these oversteps had reached the point where they could not be forgiven. One of the pillars of the US Constitution—the civilian control of the military (through the president)—was at stake.

While Truman thought he had no choice, the American public condemned him for MacArthur's dismissal. His approval rating dropped to 23 percent in April. Some Republican lawmakers discussed trying to impeach Truman.

STALEMATE AND FIERCE FIGHTING

Chinese intervention into the war drove UN forces south of the 38th parallel once again. However, they soon turned the tide of the war and once again began pushing northward. In April of 1951, UN forces retook Seoul for the second time. The front between the two opposing forces settled near the 38th parallel—the border at the beginning of the war.

UN forces would battle with KPA and Chinese armies for two long years along the 38th parallel as peace talks were held, failed, and held again. UN forces did not try advance into North Korea since a negotiated end to the conflict was the objective. However, fighting was intense and bloody throughout the period. The terrain was rugged and soldiers fought for years over isolated hills that were uninhabited. The names of the famous battles reflect the savagery of the fighting: the Battle of Heartbreak Ridge and the Battle of Bloody Ridge were fought during this time.

Soviet pilots also battled UN pilots during this period of the war. Soviet pilots and planes were first sent into the war at the end of 1950 at the request of China. This was the only direct involvement that the Soviet Union took in the fighting. In the early stages of the war, the Soviet MiG-15s were technologically superior to the outdated American fighters. However, by the end of the war American fighter jets outclassed their Soviet adversaries. Throughout the war, the Soviet Union denied taking any part in the conflict, and its pilots flew in Chinese uniforms.

ARMISTICE AT LAST

After two years of negotiations, an armistice was finally arranged to end the conflict. One of the most difficult issues to negotiate was the return of North Korean prisoners of war. The North Korean government wanted all captured soldiers to be returned. Yet many captured soldiers desired to live in South Korea rather than return north. In the end, the prisoners of the war were given the choice to decide for themselves whether or not to return to the north—where many had family—or stay in the south.

The armistice established a Demilitarized Zone (**DMZ**) between North and South Korea. It stands where the front was on the day of the armistice, which is roughly, but not exactly, at the 38th parallel. Both sides withdrew 1.2 miles (2 km) to form the buffer zone between the two countries. The borders north and south of the DMZ were fortified and heavily militarized in case of renewed hostilities.

Today, the DMZ remains heavily guarded. The governments of South Korea and North Korea have never signed a peace treaty, and tensions between the two nations remain high. American troops remain stationed in South Korea to advise the South Korean military and stand ready in case of another North Korean invasion. In recent years, North Korea has developed nuclear weapons and is currently attempting to develop long range ballistic missiles capable of carrying them around the globe. This has led to increased tensions in the region and decreased the likelihood of a final peace treaty being signed in the near future.

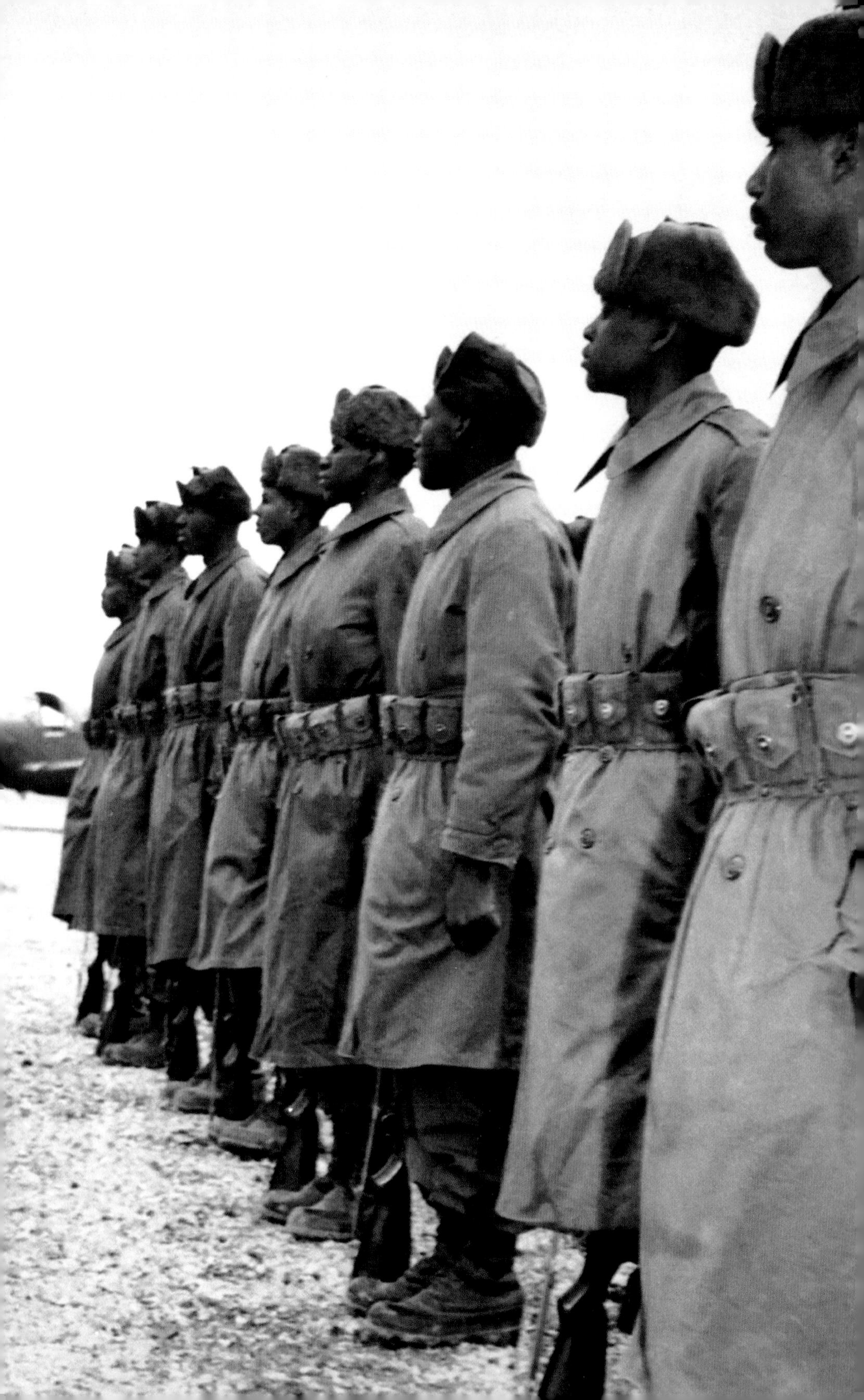

THREE

The 24th Infantry Regiment

The 24th Infantry Regiment's actions during the Korean War have been some of the most controversial in United States military history. During the war, the army blamed the race of black soldiers for any failures in their performance under fire, despite the fact that white units performed similarly. This culminated in the complete dissolution of the 24th Infantry Regiment. The unit was unceremoniously disbanded and its men integrated into other units in 1951. Many felt this was a dishonor to their service.

The reputation of the 24th Infantry Regiment remained tainted until an army report published in 1996 challenged the history of the unit. After reviewing military records and interviewing soldiers, the authors found that the performance of the 24th Infantry Regiment was similar to white regiments

Opposite: Soldiers of the 24th Infantry Regiment stand at attention.

at the time. This period of the war involved the entire US Army being ill prepared. The army was often forced to retreat because of the many organizational problems. Furthermore, the report concluded that the white chain of command failed in many ways. Racial tensions ran high and mistrust between black soldiers and white officers made effective combat operations impossible. In this chapter, we will examine the history of the 24th Infantry Regiment in the Korean War, looking at the operations it took part in as well as the heroic actions of individual soldiers.

LIFE IN JAPAN

When the Korean War began, the closest American soldiers were stationed in Japan. The United States had occupied the country since the end of World War II with General MacArthur in charge of US forces and the country as a whole. When Truman decided to intervene in the Korean War, these American troops stationed in Japan were the closest ones to the action. It was clear they would be the first to see combat in Korea and the first to try to stem the tide of the North Korean advance.

Unfortunately, the American troops occupying Japan were completely unprepared for combat. Their officers were far more concerned with keeping their men out of trouble off base than they were with preparing for the unlikely possibility that they would be deployed to a war zone. This would come back to haunt UN forces, as combat veterans from World War II who arrived later recalled that many American soldiers did not understand even basic infantry tactics. They failed to dig foxholes for cover and set up positions where no friendly forces could cover them in case of attack.

Life in Japan was easy for the 24th Infantry Regiment. Many men had girlfriends off base or lived with their families from home. Training was lax. Although their commanding officer did make sure they were physically fit, they were mentally unprepared for the savage warfare they would soon find themselves in. They were also missing basic equipment necessary for fighting. Their outdated weapons often lacked ammunition and even firing pins in some cases.

The officers and men of 24th Infantry Regiment had their doubts about their own preparedness for combat as their date to ship out to Korea drew closer and closer. They knew their equipment was faulty and mistrust between the officers and men was common. The highest-ranking black officer in the units requested that he be transferred rather than go with his men to Korea. According to the army report *Black Soldiers, White Army*, the Lieutenant Corporal said that "the regiment was neither trained nor prepared for war and that the event would be a disaster." It was a foreboding sign of things to come.

FIRST CONTACT

The 24th arrived in Pusan on July 12. They quickly rushed forward to reinforce the faltering South Korean forces retreating southward down the peninsula. On July 20, the regiment engaged the KPA for the first time at the small town of Yech'on. They managed to stop the advancing soldiers despite communication problems and confused leadership from their officers. A reporter present at Yech'on said that it was "the first sizable American ground victory in the Korean War." Back home, Congress and the press lauded the actions of the 24th in one of the few victories of that period of the war.

However, within the army, the relatively small victory at Yech'on was overshadowed by a devastating defeat at the major town of Taejeon. UN forces were forced to retreat after the loss of the city and the commanding officer of an entire American division (more than ten thousand men) was captured. Major General William F. Dean would be the highest-ranking soldier

Men in the 24th fire a howitzer at the enemy.

captured by the North Koreans—he would also receive a Medal of Honor for his daring but ultimately unsuccessful defense of Taejon. During the fighting, he personally knocked out an enemy tank with a hand grenade.

Over the next couple weeks, the 24th Infantry Regiment would take part in the Battle of Sangju. For the first time, the 24th began to falter. Some soldiers began to panic and retreat when they came under fire. Inexperienced officers were unable to control their troops and often took up positions far away from the combat rather than risk injury. The problem of stragglers reared its ugly head, as it did for many white units at the same time. Soldiers would walk away from the front lines, often abandoning their weapons and supplies, to seek safety farther from the front. Straggler lines had to be created behind the front lines. There officers would station themselves on the road and turn stragglers back towards their units. This problem was so common at the time that the names of the stragglers were not even written down—they were simply directed to return to their unit. Most did return, but often not for long.

On August 1, the 24th withdrew from around Sangju. Its ability to hold up under fire was now in question, although this was also the case of many white units at this stage in the war. By August 2, 1950, just twenty-two days after arriving in Korea, the 24th had lost 15 percent of its force. The officers had been particularly hard hit with a casualty of rate of 47 percent in those few short weeks. But it would be given no time to recover, resupply, or bolster its morale. They would take part in the **Battle of the Pusan Perimeter** that began just two days later.

Court Martial

On July 31, 1950, Leon Gilbert, an African American lieutenant, was arrested for refusing to follow a direct order from a superior officer. A white major ordered him to take twelve men and take up position on a nearby hill. Gilbert responded that the hill was overrun by North Korean soldiers and the order amounted to a suicide mission. He refused to carry it out and be responsible for the deaths of his men. He was brought before more white officers who repeated the order and warned him that he would be court martialed if he refused. He refused to change his position. He was quickly court martialed in Korea. His defense attorney argued that he was suffering from combat fatigue (now known as post-traumatic stress disorder). However, an all-white jury sentenced Gilbert to death.

The case quickly garnered publicity in the United States. The NAACP charged that the verdict was racially motivated—numerous black soldiers had been convicted of similar crimes but few white soldiers had. In the end, Truman commuted Gilbert's sentence to twenty years imprisonment. He served only five before being released. However, the conviction would tarnish the reputation of the 24th Infantry Regiment and haunt Gilbert until his death in 1999.

THE PUSAN PERIMETER

UN forces were stretched thin on the eve of the Battle of the Pusan Perimeter. They were able to block all the roads leading to Pusan. However, there were not enough men to form a continuous defensive line around the area of the Korean Peninsula still under South Korean control.

The 24th received a new commander at this stage in the war: Colonel Arthur J. Champeny. According to the report *Black Soldiers, White Army*, a reporter recalled that he addressed the soldiers under his command in the following way:

He got up and told them ... that he had been in the 88th [Division] in Italy, and at that time he had an element of the [all-black] 92d [Infantry] Division attached to him, and he said that this was the outfit that had a reputation for running, and they ran all over Italy, and he said that his observations had proved that colored people did not make good combat soldiers, and that his job down there was to change the frightened 24th into the fighting 24th.

The mistrust between officers and soldiers in the unit grew. It became clear that many white officers in the units did not trust their men to fight. The soldiers, many already unsure of themselves like most troops new to combat, received scorn rather than encouragement.

Fighting at the Pusan Perimeter raged for a month and a half. The 24th Infantry Regiment was often in the thick of it, repulsing enemy advances and attacking their positions. Eventually, the battle ended with a UN victory after the KPA was forced to withdraw due to the landing at Inchon in the north.

Like many other units during the battle, the 24th Infantry Regiment was plagued by difficulties. Poor communication and the confusion of war often led them to retreat when they should not have. The issue of stragglers leaving the

Pfc. William H. Thompson posthumously received the Medal of Honor for his heroism during the Battle of the Pusan Perimeter.

front lines was once again problematic. The resentment between many men and their white officers led to increased conflict as they often blamed one another for failures in combat. The army chain of command lost faith in the 24th Infantry Regiment to effectively launch offensives when required. Unlike similar white units, there was not a systematic attempt to replace ineffective officers and bolster morale. Their shortcomings were often ascribed to the color of their skin rather than poor leadership and a lack of confidence under fire.

Nevertheless, individual soldiers often acted heroically and fearlessly. During the Battle of the Pusan Perimeter, one soldier of the 24th received the Medal of Honor for his actions. Private First Class William Thompson single-handedly delayed an enemy assault so that his comrades could withdraw to safety. His Medal of Honor citation records his actions that day:

> *Pfc. Thompson distinguished himself by conspicuous gallantry and intrepidity above and beyond the call of duty in action against the enemy. While his platoon was reorganizing under cover of darkness, fanatical enemy forces in overwhelming strength launched a surprise attack on the unit. Pfc. Thompson set up his machine gun in the path of the onslaught and swept the enemy with withering fire, pinning them down momentarily thus permitting the remainder of his platoon to withdraw to a more tenable position. Although hit repeatedly by grenade fragments and small-arms fire, he resisted all efforts of his comrades to induce him to withdraw, steadfastly remained at his machine gun and continued to deliver deadly, accurate fire until mortally wounded by an enemy grenade. Pfc. Thompson's dauntless courage and gallant self-sacrifice reflect the highest credit on himself and uphold the esteemed traditions of military service.*

THE WAR GOES ON

During the Battle of the Pusan Perimeter, the decision was made to deactivate the 24th Infantry Regiment due to its failures in the field. This meant that its men would be distributed to unsegregated units—finally complying with Truman's order two years previously to desegregate the armed forces. However,

Sgt. Cornelius H. Charlton posthumously received the Medal of Honor for continuing to lead his men despite being critically wounded.

the 24th would fight on for nearly a year before it was possible for it be disbanded.

During this time, the regiment took part in the offensive that pushed into North Korea and the defense against the later Chinese invasion. Its performance in the field improved during this time period as its men gained valuable experience under fire and the quality of its officer corps improved.

Near the end of its career, the 24th Infantry Regiment took part in the fighting centered on the 38th parallel. Soldiers fought over rocky ridges and small hills to improve their positions and inflict losses on the enemy. It was during this fighting that the second African American soldier of the Korean War earned a Medal of Honor. Sergeant Cornelius H. Charlton was posthumously decorated after his actions on June 2, 1951. The Medal of Honor citation records his bravery that day:

> *Sgt. Charlton, a member of Company C, distinguished himself by conspicuous gallantry and intrepidity above and beyond the call of duty in action against the enemy. His platoon was attacking heavily defended hostile positions on commanding ground when the leader was wounded and evacuated. Sgt. Charlton assumed command, rallied the men, and spearheaded the assault against the hill. Personally eliminating 2 hostile positions and killing 6 of the enemy with his rifle fire and grenades, he continued up the slope until the unit suffered heavy casualties and became pinned down. Regrouping the men he led them forward only to be again hurled back by a shower of grenades. Despite a severe chest wound, Sgt. Charlton refused medical attention and led a third daring charge which carried*

★ ★ ★ ★ ★ ★ ★ ★

Jesse L. Brown

African Americans served not only in the 24th Infantry Regiment but also in other units of the army and in the other branches of the armed services. The marines, navy, and air force all underwent integration throughout the duration of the Korean War at differing speeds. One trailblazing African

Ensign Jesse L. Brown in the cockpit of an F4U Corsair

American in the military was Jesse L. Brown. In 1948, he became the first African American aviator in the US Navy. Two years later when the Korean War began, he would participate in twenty strikes on enemy forces during the first six months of the war. Flying an F4U Corsair, he **strafed** the enemy from low-altitude using the plane's cannons and rockets. This put him at risk of anti-aircraft fire from the ground.

On December 4, 1950, Brown flew in the Battle of the Chosin Reservoir. He attacked Chinese forces in defense of surrounded marines on the ground. In the fighting, his aircraft was damaged. Brown was forced to crash land behind enemy lines. He was seriously injured in the crash. His wingman Thomas J. Hudner Jr. deliberately crash landed his own aircraft next to Brown to try to free him from the wreckage, but he was not able to do so before nightfall. Trapped in his aircraft, Brown passed away that night. Brown posthumously received the Distinguished Flying Cross for his actions that day. In disregard for his own safety, he exposed himself to enemy fire to aid soldiers on the ground. Hudner would also be decorated for his daring attempt to save Brown's life. He was awarded the Medal of Honor from President Truman.

to the crest of the ridge. Observing that the remaining emplacement which had retarded the advance was situated on the reverse slope, he charged it alone, was again hit by a grenade but raked the position with a devastating fire which eliminated it and routed the defenders. The wounds received during his daring exploits resulted in his death but his indomitable courage, superb leadership, and gallant self-sacrifice reflect the highest credit upon himself the infantry, and the military service.

Despite the bravery of soldiers like Charlton, the 24th Infantry Regiment was disbanded on October 1, 1951. It was the only segregated unit to meet such a fate; most were simply integrated. The men of the regiment were allowed to rest a few days behind the front, since they had been in the thick of combat for the past seventy-two days. They were then ordered to different units to continue fighting in the war.

The end of the 24th did not merit much attention in the United States. Their legacy would suffer a period of ill-repute before being reevaluated in the 1990s. In 1995, the unit designation of the 24th Infantry Regiment was re-instituted. The new unit served during the Iraq War and is currently based in Fort Wainwright, Alaska.

In the end, it is true that discipline problems and a tendency to retreat under heavy fire plagued the 24th throughout some periods of the Korean War. However, these problems occurred in many units during the time. The army blamed only the race of the soldiers for these issues when it came to the 24th. This prevented decisive action from being taken to solve the problems the unit faced. The mistrust between officers and the men they were supposed to lead was an especially difficult problem that afflicted the 24th and not white units during the war. Under the stress of combat, this led to many breakdowns in the performance of the unit. Nevertheless, the individual soldiers of the 24th fought with exceptional bravery. Two were awarded the Medal of Honor for their selfless sacrifice to protect their brothers in arms. The 24th also performed admirably in many engagements, such as the battle at Yech'on in the opening days of the war. Their heroism is a credit to their country and their part in the Korean War helped shape the world we know today.

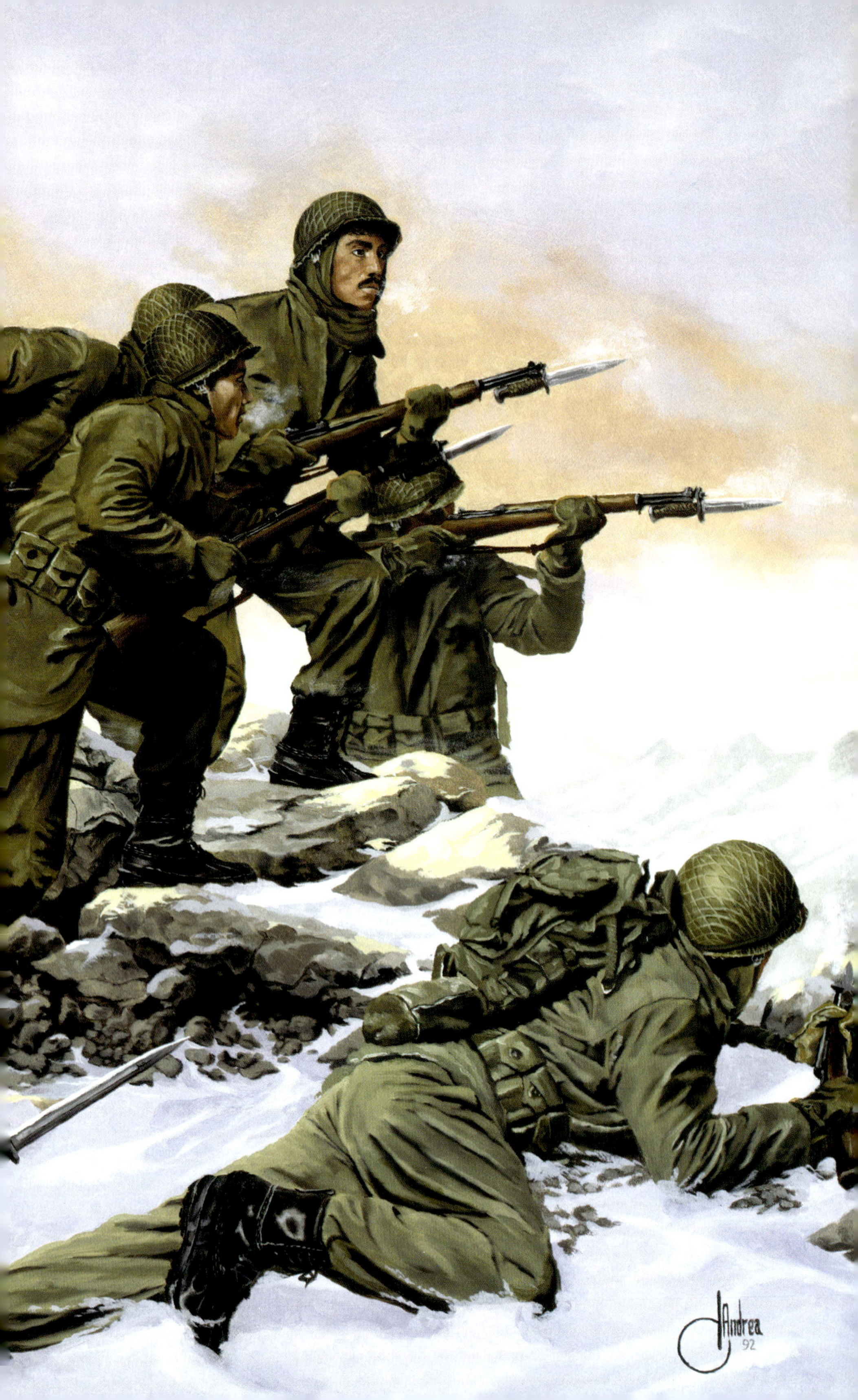

Andrea
92

FOUR

Hispanic Soldiers and Stories of Heroism

During the course of the Korean War, approximately 150,000 Hispanic Americans served in the United States Armed Forces. They served in every branch of the military but most were part of the army and marine corps. At the start of the war, some Hispanics were integrated into the armed forces, though there were still some segregated units. Unlike African American units, their segregated units were often commanded by Hispanic officers rather than white officers. By the end of the war, integration had taken place and segregated units no longer existed in the military. The daring exploits and heroism of units such as Puerto Rico's 65th Infantry Regiment continue to be a source of pride for Hispanics today.

Opposite: A famous bayonet charge by the men of the 65th Infantry Regiment during the Korean War

In this chapter, we will examine the contributions of the 65th Infantry Regiment as well as a number of individual Hispanic soldiers serving in branches outside the US Army. One of the most successful American fighter pilots was of Hispanic descent, and many Hispanics fighting in integrated units were decorated for their bravery. Their stories illustrate the great service that the 150,000 Hispanic soldiers of the Korean War performed for their country.

THE BORINQUENEERS

Puerto Rico is an island in the Caribbean with a largely Hispanic population. A former colony of Spain, it became part of the United States in 1898. Puerto Rico is an unincorporated territory of the United States. This means that Puerto Ricans are able to serve in the United States military, although they are not able to vote in presidential elections or be represented in Congress. They are also subject to the draft when it is in effect.

During both world wars and the beginning years of the Korean War, Puerto Ricans were usually segregated into their own units. The most famous of these units was the 65th Infantry Regiment, which also goes by the nickname "the Borinqueneers." Borinquen was the indigenous name of Puerto Rico before the arrival of the Spanish.

In the opening months of the Korean War, UN forces fared quite poorly. As they retreated south before the KPA, UN commanders desperately sought new troops from abroad to reinforce their lines. The 65th Infantry Regiment, stationed in Puerto Rico, was an obvious choice. On the way to Korea, it was bolstered by an additional battalion of Puerto Rican soldiers stationed in Panama at the Panama Canal. Many of

Medal of Honor recipient Master Sergeant Juan E. Negrón served in the 65th.

the soldiers of the 65th were veterans of World War II. They would prove a valuable fighting force in the early months of the war.

The Borinqueneers arrived in Korea on September 23, 1950, about three months after the start of the war and a matter of days after the Battle of the Pusan Perimeter. They took part in the UN offensive out of the Pusan Perimeter that drove the KPA back into North Korea. They fought well during the offensive; General MacArthur stated that they were an able force of the battlefield and a credit to Puerto Rico.

As UN forces advanced into North Korea, the 65th was caught up in the Battle of the Chosin Reservoir. While surrounded marine and army units desperately fought to avoid and then escape encirclement by the Chinese, the 65th fought to cover their retreat. Then, as UN forces were evacuated by the sea, the 65th protected the port in case of a Chinese assault before they themselves were evacuated. Twenty-four Silver Stars were awarded to men of the 65th for their actions in the battle.

Over the next months, the Borinqueneers were involved in a number of campaigns to halt the Chinese advance into South Korea and then to push them back out. Many individuals and units distinguished themselves by their bravery. In one notable incident, two entire battalions of Borinqueneers fixed their bayonets and charged the enemy. The action caused the Chinese to panic and flee—winning the battle. It was the last time in US military history that a battalion of soldiers participated in a bayonet charge. It is a telling anecdote of the bravery of the Borinqueneers.

On April 28, 1950, a battalion of the 65th was attacked at night by a large force of Chinese soldiers. Part of their line was breached. It appeared that the Chinese might gain an important position to the detriment of UN soldiers. However, Master Sergeant Juan E. Negrón refused to withdraw with the rest of his men and continued to fire on the advancing Chinese around him. He held his position throughout the night, inflicting heavy losses on the enemy and stopping the Chinese offensive. The next morning, fifteen enemy soldiers were found dead around his position. Negrón was awarded the Silver Star for his actions. In 2014, years after his death in 1996, Negrón would posthumously be awarded the Medal of Honor.

Outpost Kelly and Jackson Heights

Although the 65th was regarded as one of the best-performing regiments in the opening months of the war, its legacy would later be darkened. On September 18, 1952, the regiment came under attack by a vastly superior Chinese force. They lost an important position—Outpost Kelly—to the enemy. Counterattacks failed to retake the position. In October of 1952, a night assault once again seized an important mountain—Jackson Heights. Repeated counterattacks failed to recapture the heights as well.

The chain of command blamed the men of the 65th for these failures. In particular, commanders thought some men had been unwilling to engage with the enemy and in some cases refused to carry out orders that would have risked their lives in combat. As a result, 123 soldiers were court-martialed. Many were given jail sentences ranging from months to years. All the soldiers would soon be pardoned.

Today, weak leadership is generally blamed for the failure of the 65th at Outpost Kelly and Jackson Heights. Battle-hardened NCOs and officers were rotated out of the unit, leaving inexperienced men to lead the unit into battle. This coupled with supply shortages and low levels of morale led to disaster.

However, the 65th would go on to redeem itself after the defeats of late 1952. Although the top officers of the military discussed disbanding it, they would allow the unit to retrain and join the fight. During the close of the war, the 65th served with distinction at the front. It would be the last segregated unit to take part in the Korean War.

DOGFIGHTS IN MIG ALLEY

Outside the army and marines fighting on the ground, Hispanics also served their country in the navy and air force. Perhaps the most famous Hispanic to serve in the navy or air force was ace fighter pilot Manuel J. Fernandez. He participated in the fierce aerial combat that took place in the so-called "MiG Alley." Named after the Soviet fighter jet, MiG Alley referred to the northwestern corner of North Korea. Soviet jets flown by Chinese, North Korean, and Soviet pilots would take off from airfields in China to dogfight UN pilots in this region.

During the course of the Korean War, some forty American pilots achieved the status of ace. They won this distinction by destroying at least five enemy aircraft. This marked them as a cut above the typical pilot because it was a difficult feat to achieve. Manuel J. Fernandez was credited with 14.5 "kills" (pilots often ejected and survived the destruction of their aircraft). He shot down fourteen enemies singlehandedly and contributed to the destruction of another with the aid of another pilot.

Ace pilot Manuel J. Fernandez in front of an F-86 Sabre jet fighter—used in the later years of the war.

1st Lt. Baldomero Lopez climbs over the sea wall at Inchon.

Only two American pilots had more kills than Fernandez and just barely. It was especially hard during the Korean War for fighter pilots to destroy so many enemy aircraft because aces were usually pulled from Korea soon after they achieved a large number of kills. The military judged that they were more useful training rookie pilots at home for how to effectively engage the enemy than they were in the skies of Korea. This policy also aimed to prevent famous aces from being killed in combat—which would be a propaganda victory for enemies of the United States.

For his part, Fernandez wished he could have stayed in Korea longer and possibly become the top ace of the war. Nevertheless, his comrades remember him as a modest individual who would rather ensure the safety of those flying with him than earn another kill (unlike some other aces in the intense competition for kills). His prowess at the highly technical skill of hitting the enemy from far away with the cannons of his aircraft was also legendary among pilots of the war.

MARINES AWARDED THE HIGHEST HONOR

Outside the 65th Infantry Regiment, Hispanics also served bravely in integrated units throughout the war. A number in both the US Army and US Marine Corps received the highest honor—the Medal of Honor—for their actions during the war.

The US Marine Corps is one of the five branches of the US military: the others are the army, navy, air force, and coast guard. The mission of the marine corps is to be a rapid response force when world events call for quick military intervention. They also specialize in amphibious assaults. This is why it was the marines that spearheaded the landing at Inchon and not the army.

The marines enjoy a close relationship with US Navy. In fact, since 1834 they have been a part of the US Department of the navy. This close relationship is reflected in decorations awarded to marines. They wear the same variant of the Medal of Honor that members of the navy do. Despite their focus on rapid response and amphibious assault, US Marines are often called upon to engage in conventional ground combat as well. They pride themselves on accomplishing this task with deadly efficiency. The famous Marine saying that "Every Marine a rifleman" reflects the importance placed on infantry combat.

A Picture of Courage

One of the most famous photographs of the Korean War comes from the marine landing at Inchon. In the picture, a marine can be seen climbing over the sea wall, exposing himself to enemy fire and advancing on the enemy. Although the photographer did not know it at the time, he had photographed Medal of Honor recipient Lieutenant Baldomero Lopez minutes before he gave his life for his comrades.

Lopez and his men were confronted by strong enemy fortifications on the other side of the sea wall. They fought to advance and form a beachhead for the soldiers following behind them. Coming upon an enemy **pillbox**, Lopez pulled the pin from a grenade and prepared to throw it inside. Before he could do so, he was hit by a burst of **automatic fire** in his chest and shoulder. The grenade fell from his hand and rolled away toward the men under his command. Despite his grievous wounds, Lopez crawled after the grenade. Too weak to grasp hold of the grenade, he used his arm to sweep it under his body. This action ensured Lopez's own death, but it shielded his comrades from the blast of the grenade.

Lopez made the ultimate sacrifice to protect his men from harm. He would posthumously be awarded the Medal of Honor. Today, a naval vessel also bears his name. A picture of Lopez along with his Medal of Honor citation hang outside his old room at the US Naval Academy.

Eugene Arnold Obregon

After the landing at Inchon, the marines advanced on Seoul and took the city in the Second Battle of Seoul. Fighting was fierce as UN soldiers were forced the clear the KPA out of the city street by street and house by house. Hundreds of soldiers gave their lives to retake the city and help turn the tide of the war. One marine—Eugene Arnold Obregon—gave his life to rescue a wounded marine caught in the open. His Medal of Honor citation records his heroic actions that day:

> *While serving as an ammunition carrier of a machine gun squad in a marine rifle company which was temporarily pinned down by hostile fire, Pfc. Obregon observed a fellow marine fall wounded in the line of fire. Armed only with a pistol, he unhesitating dashed from his covered position to the side of the casualty. Firing his pistol with 1 hand as he ran, he grasped his comrade by the arm with his other hand and, despite the great peril to himself dragged him to the side of the road. Still under enemy fire, he was bandaging the man's wounds when hostile troops of approximately platoon strength*

Navajo Code Talkers

Native Americans also served their country bravely during the Korean War. One of the most famous groups was the Navajo code talkers. Although they are most often remembered for their service during World War II, they also operated during the Korean War. Members of the Navajo tribe used their unique

Navajo code talkers transmit encoded messages in the Pacific theater of World War II.

language to create a code on the US military's behalf during World War II. This allowed them to securely communicate messages over a radio during combat. Unencrypted messages could be picked up by the enemy and taken advantage of, but the Navajo code was indecipherable. It proved to be a valuable asset during both World War II and the Korean War.

The Navajo who invented the code were roughly treated by the United States government before their service. Sent to Native American boarding schools, their use of Navajo language was often punished harshly when they were children. But the language would prove a valuable commodity for their country when they grew up. Even after the end of World War II, many Native Americans returned to homes that would not even allow them to vote in elections due to their heritage. However, they did not let this unfair treatment prevent them from serving their country with honor and bravery. The last living Navajo code talker passed away in 2014, but their service is still remembered and celebrated by the United States.

*began advancing toward his position. Quickly seizing the wounded marine's **carbine**, he placed his own body as a shield in front of him and lay there firing accurately and effectively into the hostile group until he himself was fatally wounded by enemy machine gun fire. By his courageous fighting spirit, fortitude, and loyal devotion to duty, Pfc. Obregon enabled his fellow marines to rescue the wounded man and aided essentially in repelling the attack, thereby sustaining and enhancing the highest traditions of the U.S. Naval Service. He gallantly gave his life for his country.*

The wounded Marine, Bert M. Johnson, survived due to the selfless actions of Obregon.

Ambrosio Guillen

Even though armistice negotiations were taking place, fighting was intense until the final day of the war. On July 25, 1953, Staff Sergeant Ambrosio Guillen took part in the defense of an outpost in front of UN lines. Attacked by a force that vastly outnumbered his own, Guillen left cover and exposed himself to enemy fire to lead his platoon. His bravery rallied his men and allowed them to repulse the enemy offensive. Even after Guillen was critically wounded, he stayed in combat to direct his men in battle and refused to be evacuated so that his wounds could be treated. He lost his life due to the wounds he received in the battle. His example of courage under fire and leadership allowed his men to hold their position.

Two days after Staff Sergeant Guillen's heroic actions, the Korean War would come to an end. The actions of Hispanic soldiers like Guillen contributed to the outcome of the war and the creation of a democratic South Korea. Despite the segregation and racism they faced at home, they served their country bravely in combat. Their actions in the adverse conditions of the war are a credit to their country. It's a legacy that all Americans should be proud of.

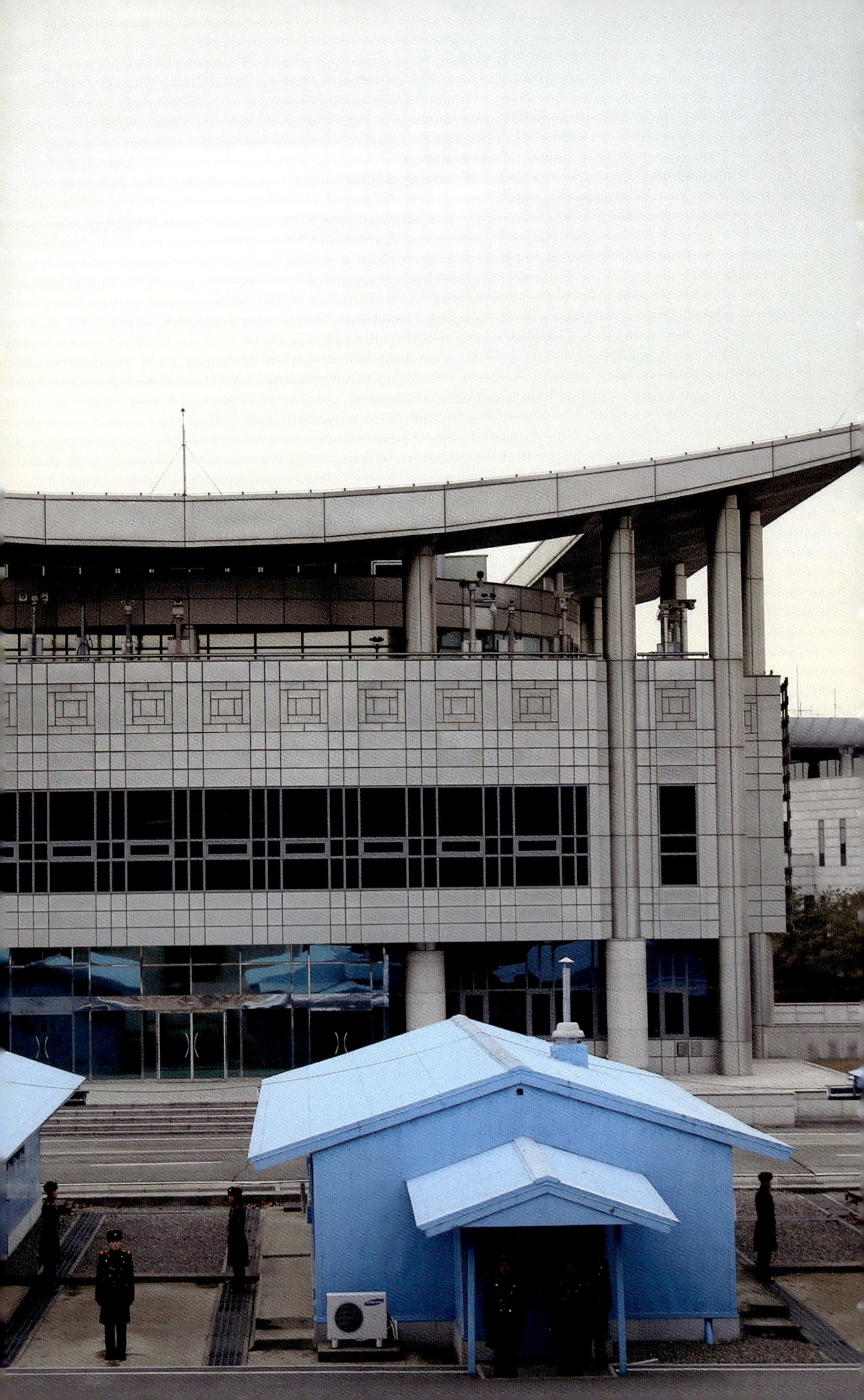

FIVE

Changing Times

With the end of the Korean War, veterans returned home to the United States and the other countries from which UN troops came. Unlike at the end of World War II, massive parades and celebrations did not mark their return. Neither did they face the protests and scorn that returning Vietnam veterans would experience decades later. Instead, the end of the Korean War occasioned relatively little attention from the American public. Today, the war is still called "the Forgotten War" and for good reason.

It would be forty-two years between the end of the war and the inauguration of the Korean War Veterans Memorial in Washington, DC. For comparison, the Vietnam Veterans Memorial opened just seven years after the end of that war. The courage and heroism of a generation of soldiers in Korea was largely ignored in their own country. But their sacrifice has never been forgotten in South Korea. Every year since

Opposite: The North Korean side of the border between the two Koreas

1975, groups of veterans and their families visit South Korea under the Revisit Korea program. The Korean government pays for part of their travel expenses and throws events to honor their part in making South Korea the free, democratic nation it is today.

AN ELUSIVE PEACE

The legacy of the Korean War has been particularly problematic because there is still no formal peace treaty. The armistice spells out a ceasefire but not lasting terms for peace. The North Korean regime has been isolated since the end of the war. Its harsh treatment toward its own citizens has brought about international condemnation. While the people of North Korea suffer from poverty and often even starvation, the government continues to spend large sums on the military and luxuries for government officials.

The Korean DMZ still stretches across the Korean Peninsula and is occasionally the site of violence between the two countries. In 1976, more than twenty years after the end of the war, two American soldiers died in the DMZ while taking part in an effort to prune a tree that was blocking visibility from a military outpost. During a confrontation, they were killed by North Korean soldiers wielding axes. These were the last American deaths attributed to the North Koreans, but violence has never completely stopped.

In 2010, North Korean artillery bombarded the South Korean island of Yeonpyeong. Two South Korean civilians were killed and many others were wounded. Two South Korean military personnel stationed on the island also lost their lives in the bombardment. This is only the latest attack by North

Korea. Many others preceded it and the conflict between North and South Korea is still ongoing.

In recent years, a final peace treaty has been impossible because of the North Korean nuclear program. In 2006, North Korea succeeded in detonating a nuclear bomb. They are now estimated to have a number of nuclear bombs stockpiled. (They lack the capability to deliver them via long-range missiles, though.) North Korea views their nuclear weapons as insurance against any large-scale military action against them. The United States and most other countries view their nuclear program as a threat to global stability and peace.

The United States has demanded that North Korea dismantle their nuclear program before serious peace talks begin—a demand that North Korea has consistently refused. Due to its nuclear program, North Korea suffers under some of the most stringent economic sanctions in the world today. These restrict its ability to export goods and earn money with which to pursue further nuclear developments. China has been the primary supporter of North Korea since the end of the Korean War. It has sent aid to the country and been one of the few countries to keep business ties with the internationally shunned government of North Korea. But even the Chinese government's attitude toward North Korea has been hardening in recent years, as North Korea's regime acts ever more erratically.

Under President Obama, the United States and North Korea briefly considered peace talks. However, the nuclear issue derailed them before they could begin. Currently, it does not look likely that a peace treaty will be signed in the near future, although some activist groups are still campaigning for it.

UNEQUAL RECOGNITION

While some minority soldiers were awarded with military decorations during the Korean War, many others who were worthy were not. This unequal treatment of minorities is not surprising given the racial climate of the times. Many individual officers harbored racist sentiments. It was easy for them to not recommend soldiers for decorations even if their heroic actions were documented.

In 2002, the United States Congress required the Pentagon to review the files of Hispanic and Jewish soldiers who might not have been awarded the Medal of Honor due to racial discrimination. The review took twelve years to complete. The US Army examined the records relating to the award of 6,505 Distinguished Service Crosses (the second highest honor) to see if any should be upgraded to the Medal of Honor. In the end, the army determined that twenty-four soldiers who deserved to receive the Medal of Honor had not been awarded it. Nine of these veterans fought in the Korean War, seven in World War II, and eight in the Vietnam War.

One Jewish soldier to receive the Medal of Honor from this review was Leonard M. Kravitz, the uncle and namesake of the famous singer Lenny Kravitz. Lenny Kravitz's sister received the award from President Obama on her uncle's behalf. Private First Class Kravitz was credited with allowing his company to withdraw when they were overwhelmingly outnumbered during a battle with the enemy. After a machine gunner was killed in action, Kravitz took up the weapon and inflicted devastating losses on the charging enemy. This caused the attackers to focus on his position while he shouted for his comrades to

President Obama presents the Medal of Honor to Pfc. Kravitz's niece.

take the opportunity to fall back. As the attackers continued to advance, Kravitz remained at his post to slow down the attack and buy time for his fellow soldiers. When the position was later retaken, Kravitz's remains were found at the machine gun surrounded by dead enemy soldiers. He had held his position until the last possible moment.

A childhood friend of Kravitz, Mitch Libman, later read his Distinguished Service Cross citation and thought it was clearly worthy of a Medal of Honor. Libman campaigned on

Changing Times

his friend's behalf to have the situation reviewed by the army. He suspected it was the fact that Kravitz was a Jew that had prevented him from receiving the highest honor possible. In the end, his campaign would help lead the Congressional act that called for a review of all Hispanic and Jewish citations in 2002 and ultimately ended with Kravitz receiving the Medal of Honor.

Yet the battle for recognition by minority soldiers for their actions in the Korean War has still not come to an end. While nine Korean War veterans were fittingly awarded the Medal of Honor in 2014, others still argue that they were passed over due to their race and the discriminatory policies and racist officers of the era.

Lieutenant Colonel Charles M. Bussey is one such African American soldier who recalled the racially charged atmosphere of his time in Korea. He believed it had an effect on his recommendation for military decorations. On July 20, 1950, at the Battle of Yech'on, Bussey prevented advancing KPA forces from flanking the 24th Infantry Regiment. Passing by a firefight, Bussey observed that enemy soldiers were flanking American forces. He found two nearby truck drivers and two machine guns and took up position on a nearby hill. Pouring machine gun fire into the enemy, he was credited with killing 258 of them, turning the tide of the engagement.

After the battle, he was only awarded the Silver Star—the third-highest military decoration. According to Bussey, the general who gave it to him told him to expect the Medal of Honor at a later date (it is a longer process to receive the higher award). But Bussey's commanding officer told him that he would never recommend him for the Medal of Honor due to his race. He told Bussey that he did not want Bussey to become a Jackie Robinson and inspire other African Americans. In a glimpse into the racist attitudes of the time, Bussey recalled that before this frank conversation he often fraternized with this officer. They had shared drinks many nights before.

Bussey believed this overtly racist officer prevented him from receiving the Medal of Honor. After the war, Bussey would finish out a distinguished military career with the army. Yet he would never receive the Medal of Honor. He died in 2004, still fighting for recognition. He did not desire the medal as a personal honor, but as a way to inspire young African Americans who were considering joining the military. In an interview with the *New York Times* he stated, "But the importance is that if I can earn one of these, other kids can earn one as well. I want to be able to tell them that they can be all that they can be in the Army and that the service is grateful. But I can't do that now."

AN END TO SEPARATE BUT EQUAL

Like other veterans, minority soldiers of the Korean War returned home to relative obscurity. Their sacrifices and heroism were often ignored. But unlike other veterans, they also had to contend with racial inequality, segregation, and discrimination. At the end of the war, segregation was still the law of the land throughout much of the United States. A Supreme Court decision in 1896, *Plessy v. Ferguson*, had upheld racial segregation under the doctrine of "separate but equal." This allowed schools and other government facilities to discriminate against African Americans and other minorities by providing them separate services than whites. In theory, these services were supposed

Thurgood Marshall after being appointed to the Supreme Court

to be of equal quality. In practice, they were almost always far inferior. Schools for African Americans generally received only a fraction of the funding and resources of schools for whites. But this situation was about to change.

On May 17, 1954, less than a year after the end of the Korean War, the US Supreme Court decided one of the most important cases in American history: *Brown v. Board of Education.*

The case was on behalf of a number of students who argued that the segregated schools they went to were in fact unequal. In a unanimous decision, the Supreme Court agreed with the students and rejected continued racial segregation in American schools. Chief Justice Earl Warren's decision said the following, in part:

> We conclude that, in the field of public education, the doctrine of "separate but equal" has no place. Separate educational facilities are inherently unequal. Therefore, we hold that the plaintiffs and others similarly situated for whom the actions have been brought are, by reason of the segregation complained of, deprived of the equal protection of the laws guaranteed by the Fourteenth Amendment.

Overnight, a policy that had discriminated against minorities for generations was overturned by the stroke of a pen.

Brown v. Board of Education was not a matter of chance. The NAACP Legal Defense Fund had been working tirelessly for decades to challenge racial segregation in the courts. Thurgood Marshall, an African American lawyer from Maryland, was a leading member of the organization. He argued *Brown v. Board of Education* before the Supreme Court, but it was not his first successful case. He had won earlier victories against segregation in universities. Throughout his long career, Marshall would argue thirty-cases before the Supreme Court and emerge victorious in twenty-nine of them. He struck many important blows against the system of racial discrimination and segregation that existed at that time. His own extremely successful career served as an inspiration to African Americans around the country. In 1967,

Marshall himself was appointed to the US Supreme Court. He was the first African American to sit on the court.

THE CIVIL RIGHTS MOVEMENT

Brown v. Board of Education is often cited as the beginning of the Civil Rights Movement that would stretch from 1954 to 1968. It was a turbulent time, overlapping with the beginning of the Vietnam War. It also saw widespread civil unrest, as African Americans peacefully protested their unfair treatment while the response of law enforcement was sometimes less than peaceful. Race riots, often inspired by the rough treatment of African Americans, also broke out in many cities. Some fringe African American groups called for violent, rather than nonviolent, resistance.

The leaders of the Civil Rights Movement are remembered for their deep belief in peaceful, nonviolent protest, even in the face of violent suppression. Their efforts culminated in a series of important pieces of legislation that expanded the rights of minorities in the United States. The Voting Rights Act of 1965 sought to end the disenfranchisement of African Americans (primarily in the South). It ended the Jim Crow laws that had tried to circumvent giving African Americans the right to vote by means such as poll taxes and literacy tests (which often did not require whites to pass them). The Civil Rights Act of 1968 also guaranteed equal housing opportunities. It was no longer possible to refuse to sell or rent housing to people based on their gender, race, or religion.

The Civil Rights Movement took place over many years in many different places, so there was no one leader of the movement. However, many African Americans rose to

Martin Luther King Jr. gained notoriety during the Montgomery Bus Boycott of 1955 and 1956.

prominence during this time. They are now household names. Their heroic actions are remembered and celebrated across the United States.

Martin Luther King Jr.

Perhaps the most famous civil rights leader was Reverend Martin Luther King Jr. King was a Baptist minister who rose to prominence in the Civil Rights Movement. He was an important leader of the Montgomery Bus Boycott, which lasted for more than a year between December of 1955 and 1956. The boycott began after Rosa Parks refused to move from her seat when a bus driver ordered her to move so that white passengers could sit. Rather than abide by the stringent Jim Crow laws

Martin Luther King Jr. leading the March on Washington

that dictated where African American passengers could sit on city buses, African Americans around the city walked or found other means of transportation. After the Supreme Court ruled against the discriminatory laws, Montgomery finally changed them, ending the boycott. King's role in organizing and being a spokesperson for the boycott made him a national figure.

In 1963, the historic March on Washington for Jobs and Freedom took place. Hundreds of thousands of protesters marched in Washington, DC. They wanted an end to segregation and racism as well as greater economic opportunity. King delivered the most famous speech of the event, now known as "I Have a Dream." His words would echo across the nation. His passionate denunciation of racism is a defining moment in American history.

King's influential leadership came to an end on April 4, 1968. Just thirty-nine years old, he was assassinated as a result of his activism. But the Civil Rights Movement would live on, and his dream of a world without racism continues to this day.

OLD SOLDIERS NEVER DIE, THEY JUST FADE AWAY

After General MacArthur's dismissal, he gave a farewell address to Congress. He ended with a quotation from an old army song, "old soldiers never die, they just fade away." MacArthur did just that, largely shunning the public eye after being a possible candidate for the presidency in 1952.

Shamefully, the more than six million veterans of the Korean War have also faded away from public awareness. They answered their country's call to be on the front lines of the fight against communism. However, their war never garnered

The Vietnam War

Twelve years after the end of the Korean War, the first American combat troops began pouring into Vietnam. Once again, the United States would commit its own soldiers to try to stem the spread of communism across Asia. This time the effort would fail. Vietnam would eventually be reunited under communist control after an American withdrawal. But the Vietnam War would weigh heavily on the country for six long years. It was the first war where American troops were completely desegregated from the beginning of the conflict until its end. However, it was not free from racial inequality. African Americans were drafted in larger numbers than whites. Furthermore, they were

A protest against the Vietnam War in New York City

more likely to die in combat due to their assignment to the most dangerous tasks in the military.

Civil rights leaders like Martin Luther King Jr. decried the American involvement in Vietnam. He gave a powerful speech in 1967 which outlined his own feelings towards the war:

> It became clear to me that the war was doing far more than devastating the hopes of the poor at home. It was sending their sons and their brothers and their husbands to fight and to die in extraordinarily high proportions relative to the rest of the population. We were taking the black young men who had been crippled by our society and sending them eight thousand miles away to guarantee liberties in Southeast Asia which they had not found in southwest Georgia and East Harlem.

The struggle for civil rights and peace in Vietnam would become intermingled.

the same level of attention as World War II or the Vietnam War. Their heroism and bravery, recorded in the many military decorations awarded during the conflict, is often forgotten by the country they served.

Many of the soldiers who fought in the Korean War belonged to minority groups within the United States. Their service in a time when they were usually treated like second-class citizens is a testament to their patriotism and deep sense of duty. They fought to preserve democracy and freedom in Asia when true freedom at home was often out of reach for themselves and their communities. As we have seen, many minority soldiers went above and beyond the call of duty in combat. Some gave their lives for their country and their comrades. Many received military decorations that recognized their sacrifices and recorded their heroic deeds for future generations to look back on and honor their legacy.

The Korean War ended near the place it began—the 38th parallel. But that does not mean the war was for nothing. On July 27, 2013, the sixtieth anniversary of the armistice of the Korean War, President Obama spoke the following words about the place of the Korean War in history:

> *Freedom is not free. And in Korea, no one paid a heavier price than those who gave all—36,574 American patriots, and, among our allies, more than one million of our South Korean friends—soldiers and civilians. That July day, when the fighting finally ended, not far from where it began, some suggested this sacrifice had been for naught, and they summed it up with a phrase—"die for a tie ... But here, today, we can say with confidence*

that war was no tie. Korea was a victory. When 50 million South Koreans live in freedom—a vibrant democracy, one of the world's most dynamic economies, in stark contrast to the repression and poverty of the North— that's a victory; that's your legacy.

These words remain true today. While the Korean War is still "the Forgotten War," the consequences of it are still felt by millions of Koreans every day. And without the contributions of minority soldiers, the outcome could have been much different.

Glossary

annex To add foreign territory to a country; victorious powers in a war often annex part or the entirety of the defeated country.

automatic fire Shots fired from an automatic weapon. Automatic weapons fire continuously while the trigger is pulled. Examples include machine guns and assault rifles.

Battle of the Chosin Reservoir An important battle that lasted from November 26 to December 13, 1950. Chinese forces succeeded in pushing back UN forces, but the Chinese soldiers suffered immense losses and were unable to achieve their objective of eliminating a large group of surrounded UN soldiers. The men—mostly US Marines—were able to fight their way out of encirclement.

Battle of the Pusan Perimeter A key battle of the war that took place between August 4 and September 18, 1950. UN forces were able to stop the KPA offensive and retain a foothold on the Korean Peninsula around the port city of Pusan.

carbine A firearm that is shorter than a rifle. Due to its size, a carbine is often less accurate than a rifle, but it's better suited to close quarter operations.

casualties Soldiers who are unable to continue taking part in the fighting due to either wounds, capture, or death.

containment A key American strategy of the Cold War; the United States aimed to contain communism and stop its spread around the world but not directly assault the Soviet Union or her allies. The Korean War was the first time the United States committed soldiers on the ground to further this policy.

disenfranchisement Having taken away of the right to vote from someone or some group of people.

DMZ Demilitarized Zone; an area wherein no soldiers or military equipment is allowed.

Executive Order No. 9981 Issued by President Truman on July 26, 1948, this executive order officially ordered the desegregation of the US armed forces and an end to racial inequality. However, it would not be fully implemented until the end of the Korean War in 1953.

Great Migration The wide-scale movement of African Americans from the rural South to cities in the North between 1916 and 1970.

Inchon The port city close to Seoul where UN forces landed in the early days of the war. Today, it is spelled Incheon and is home the South Korea's largest airport.

Jim Crow laws Laws that enforced the system of racial segregation present in the South between the 1870s and 1960s.

KPA Korean People's Army; the military force of North Korea during the Korean War and today.

Mendez v. Westminster The first court case decided against segregation in 1946. It found that Mexican children could not be sent to separate schools from white children due to their race.

NAACP The National Association for the Advancement of Colored People; founded in 1909, the organization played a key role in the fight against racial segregation.

nuclear deterrence The idea that possessing nuclear weapons will dissuade other countries from using nuclear weapons since retaliation would be devastating.

pillbox A small, defensive structure that is generally made of concrete. Soldiers inside fire weapons through narrow windows that protect them from enemy fire.

proxy war A war fought by two powers that do not directly engage each other with their armed forces. Instead, they support third parties in a conflict to further their own aims.

Pusan The second most important city of South Korea after Seoul. It is also the largest port city in Korea and was the landing place of most UN troops in the Korean War. It gave its name to the Pusan Perimeter. Today, the city is called Busan.

Pyongyang The capital city of North Korea. Today, it is spelled Pyeongyang in English.

routed To have caused a fighting force to retreat in disorder.

Seoul The capital of South Korea. It fell and was retaken twice during the Korean War and today more than half of South Korea's population lives in the city or its surrounding area.

sphere of influence A term in international relations that denotes one country has a high level of influence over another country. During the Cold War, most of Eastern Europe was within the sphere of influence of the Soviet Union.

strafe To attack troops or vehicles on the ground from a low-flying aircraft using machine guns or cannons—not bombs.

38th parallel The border between North and South Korea before the outbreak of the Korean War. The modern-day border is often still referred to as the 38th parallel, even though it is not precisely at the line.

Truman Doctrine The name given to President Truman's foreign policy that involved heavily supporting foreign governments who were threatened by the expansion of the Soviet Union.

UN United Nations; an international organization that seeks to prevent wars and increase the cooperation between countries. Its military forces, primarily made up of Americans, provided large numbers of troops to the South Korean cause during the Korean War.

Bibliography

Astor, Gerald. *The Right to Fight: A History of African Americans in the Military.* Boston: Da Capo Press, 2011.

Bussey, Charles M. *Firefight at Yechon: Courage and Racism in the Korean War.* Lincoln, NE: University of Nebraska Press, 2004.

Cho, Jae-hyon. "Data Show Park Chung-hee Pledged Allegiance to Japanese Army." *Korea Times,* November 6, 2009. http://www.koreatimes.co.kr/www/news/people/2013/08/178_55034.html.

Cleaver, Thomas McKelvey. "The US Marine Corps' Finest Hour—Battle of the Chosin Reservoir." Osprey Publishing Blog, July 29, 2016. https://ospreypublishing.com/blog/battle_of_the_chosin_reservoir/.

Dudziak, Mary L. *Cold War Civil Rights: Race and the Image of American Democracy.* Princeton: Princeton University Press, 2011.

Echávarri, Fernanda, and Marlon Bishop. "'No Mexicans Allowed:' School Segregation in the Southwest." Latino USA, March 11, 2016. http://latinousa.org/2016/03/11/no-mexicans-allowed-school-segregation-in-the-southwest/.

Florence Times. "Negro Is Sentenced to Die for $1.95 Robbery." August 20, 1958. https://news.google.com/ newspapers?nid= ie8Y0QrpMWAC&dat=19580820&printsec=frontpage&hl=en.

Florido, Adrian. "Mass Deportation May Sound Unlikely, But It's Happened Before." NPR, September 8, 2015. http://www.npr.org/sections/codeswitch/2015/09/08/437579834/mass-deportation-may-sound-unlikely-but-its-happened-before.

Fox, Margalit. "Chester Nez, 93, Dies: Navajo Words Washed from Mouth Helped Win the War." *New York Times,* June 5, 2014. https://www.nytimes.com/2014/06/06/us/chester-nez-dies-at-93-his-native-tongue-helped-to-win-a-war-of-words.html?_r=0.

King, Martin Luther. "Statement Delivered at the Prayer Pilgrimage Protesting the Electrocution of Jeremiah Reeves." Speech at Montgomery, AL, April 6, 1958. https://swap.stanford.edu/20141218225520/http://mlk-kpp01.stanford.edu/primarydocuments/Vol4/6-Apr-1958_JeremiahReevesStatement.pdf.

———. *Stride toward Freedom: The Montgomery Story.* Boston: Beacon Press, 2010.

Latson, Jennifer. "How Emmett Till's Murder Changed the World." *Time,* August 28, 2015. http://time.com/4008545/emmett-till-history/.

Schlesinger, Robert. "Truman Firing of MacArthur Hurt Approval Rating But Saved War with Red China." *U.S. News & World Report,* April 9, 2009. http://www.usnews.com/opinion/articles/2009/04/09/truman-firing-of-macarthur-hurt-approval-rating-but-saved-war-with-red-china.

Smith, Charles R. Jr. *U.S. Marines in the Korean War.* Quantico, VA: US Marine Corps History Division, 2007.

Van West, Carroll. "Columbia Race Riot, 1946." *Tennessee Encyclopedia of Culture and History,* January 1, 2010. http://tennesseeencyclopedia.net/entry.php?rec=296.

Villahermosa, Gilberto N. *Honor and Fidelity: The 65th Infantry in Korea,* 1950–1953. Washington, DC: Center of Military History, 2009.

Vogel, Steve. "Unprepared to Fight." *Washington Post,* June 19, 2000. https://www.washingtonpost.com/archive/local/2000/06/19/unprepared-to-fight/ea8f34fe-794b-4085-b805-b67140b8e6a4/?utm_term=.03414f0563b4.

Watras, Joseph. "Progressive Education and Native American Schools, 1929–1950." *Educational Foundations* 18 (Summer–Fall 2004): 81–204.

Werrell, Kenneth. *Sabres over MiG Alley: The F-87 and the Battle for Air Superiority over Korea.* Annapolis: Naval Institute Press, 2005.

Further Information

Websites

American Experience: The Korean War
http://www.pbs.org/wgbh/amex/macarthur/maps/koreatxt.html

PBS presents the history of the Korean War with maps illustrating the movement of forces.

Civil Rights Chronology
http://www.civilrights.org/resources/civilrights101/chronology.html?referrer=https://www.google.com/

Explore a chronology of important events in the history of civil rights in the United States.

Hispanics in the US Army
https://www.army.mil/hispanics/history.html

Learn more about the history of Hispanics in the US Army during a number of conflicts, including the Korean War.

24th Infantry Regiment (Deuce Four)
https://www.25thida.org/units/infantry/24th-infantry-regiment/

Read an in-depth history of the 24th Infantry Regiment on the website of the 25th Infantry Division Association (the division that is now home to the 24th).

Books

Halberstam, David. *The Coldest Winter: America and the Korean War.* New York: Hachette Books, 2008.

Harris, W. W. *Puerto Rico's Fighting 65th U.S. Infantry: From San Juan to Chorwan.* New York: Presidio Press, 2001.

Nez, Chester. *Code Talker: The First and Only Memoir by One of the Original Navajo Code Talkers of WWII.* New York City: Berkley Books, 2012.

Posey, Edward L. *The US Army's First, Last, and Only All-Black Rangers: The 2d Ranger Infantry Company (Airborne) in the Korean War, 1950–1951.* El Dorado Hills, CA: Savas Beatie, 2011.

Videos

"The Battle of Chosin"
https://www.youtube.com/watch?v=zYfWhb_YNEA

PBS presents a documentary on the Battle of the Chosin Reservoir that includes interviews of the soldiers and footage of Korea.

"General MacArthur"
http://www.history.com/topics/korean-war/videos/douglas-macarthur

The History Channel provides a look at General MacArthur's turbulent career in the military.

Index

Page numbers in **boldface** are illustrations. Entries in **boldface** are glossary terms.

ace, 70, 73

African American, 7, 11–16, 18–25, 54, 59–61, 65, 86–94

amphibious, 35, 73–74

annex, 29

armistice, 46, 78, 82, 96

assimilation, 18–19

automatic fire, 74

Brown v. Board of Education, 23, 88–90

Brown, Jesse L., 60–61, **60**

Bussey, Charles M., 86–87

carbine, 78

casualties, 22, 34, 40, 53, 59, 75

Champeny, Arthur J., 55

Charlton, Cornelius H., **58**, 59, 62

China, 6, 29, 32, 37–41, 43, 45–46, 59, 68–70, 83

Chosin Reservoir, Battle of, 39, 41, 61, 68

Civil Rights Movement, 25, 90, 92–93

Cold War, 21, 24, 27–29, 31–32

Colombia Race Riot of 1946, 16

communism, 21, 24, 27, 32, 41, 93

containment, 32

deportation, 20

disenfranchisement, 12, 90

DMZ, 46, 82

Executive Order No. 9981, 25

Fernandez, Manuel J., 70, **71**, 73

Forgotten War, 6, 9, 81, 96–97

Gilbert, Leon, 54

Great Migration, 13

Guillen, Ambrosio, 78–79

Hispanic Americans, 7, 19–20, 65–66, 70, 73, 78, 84, 86

Hudner Jr., Thomas J., 61

Inchon, 34–35, 37, 55, 74–75

Jim Crow laws, 11–13, 90, 92

King Jr., Martin Luther, 15, **91**, 92–93, **92**, 95

KPA, 5, 33–37, 51, 55, 66, 68, 75, 86

Kravitz, Leonard M., 84–86

Ku Klux Klan, 13

Lopez, Baldomero, 72, 74–75

lynchings, 13–14, 16, 24

MacArthur, Douglas, 35, 37–38, 41, 43, **44**, 45, 50, 68, 93

Marshall, Thurgood, **88**, 89–90

Medal of Honor, 9, 40, 53, 57, 59, 61, 63, 69, 73–75, 84–87

Mendez v. Westminster, 20

NAACP, 18, 54, 89

Native Americans, 7, 18–19, 76–77

Navajo code talkers, 76–77

Negrón, Juan E., **67**, 69

North Atlantic Treaty Organization (NATO), 28

nuclear deterrence, 33

nuclear program, 83

Obregon, Eugene Arnold, 75, 78

Osan, Battle of, 33–34

Park Chung Hee, 30

pillbox, 74

propaganda, 21, 73

proxy war, 27, 33

Pusan, 34–36, 51

Pusan Perimeter, Battle of, 53–55, 57–58, 68

Pyongyang, 37, 43

race riots, 16, 90

racial violence, 11, 13, 20, 24

Reeves, Jeremiah, 15–16

Robinson, Jackie, 16–18, **17**

routed, 37, 62

Sangju, Battle of, 53

segregation, 9, 11–12, 16–20, 25, 58, 62, 65–66, 70, 79, 87, 89, 93

Seoul, 5–6, 33, 35, 45, 75

Seoul, Second Battle of, 35, 75

Silver Star, 68–69, 86

65th Infantry Regiment, 65–66, 68–70, 73

Soviet Union, 21, 24, 27–29, 32–33, 37–38, 41, 43, 46, 70

sphere of influence, 28

strafe, 61

stragglers, 53, 55

Termination Policy, 18–19

38th parallel, 37, 45–46, 59, 96

Thompson, William, **56**, 57

Till, Emmett, 13–14, **13**

Truman Doctrine, 32

Truman, President Harry S., 5, 24–25, 32, 35, 37, 41, 43, 45, 50, 54, 58

Tuskegee Airmen, 23

Tuskegee Institute, 13

24th Infantry Regiment, 7, 9, 49–51, 53–59, 62–63, 86

UN, 5, 32, 34–35, 37–38, 40–41, 43, 45–46, 50, 52, 55, 66, 68–70, 75, 78, 81

US Marine Corps, 40, 60–61, 65, 68, 70, 73–75, 78

Vietnam War, 6, 27, 81, 84, 90, 94–96

Wilson, Jimmy, 21, 24

World War II, 6, 20, 22–23, 25, 28–30, 33, 35, 50, 68, 76–77, 81, 84, 96

Yalu River, 37–38

Yech'on, Battle of, 51–52, 63, 86

Zoot Suit Riots, 20

About the Author

Derek Miller is a writer and educator from Salisbury, Maryland. Miller's books include Fighting for Their Country: *Minority Soldiers Fighting in World War I,* among others. In his free time, he enjoys researching topics in history and traveling with his wife. South Korea is one of his favorite places to travel.